SKELTON *at* 60

edited by
Barbara E. Turner

The Porcupine's Quill

Published by the Porcupine's Quill, Inc., 68 Main Street, Erin, Ontario NOB 1TO, with financial assistance from the Ontario Arts Council and the Canada Council.

Distributed in Canada and the United States by Firefly Books Ltd., 3520 Pharmacy Avenue, Unit 1C, Scarborough, Ontario M1W 2T8.

Some of the poems appearing here have been previously published: 'Coast to Coast' (1. WEST) by Fleur Adcock in the *Honest Ulsterman*, no. 75; 'Suddenly Glancing Up From My Book' by John Barton in *Waves*; 'The Rust-Red Grown Beds' by Lala Heine-Koehn in *Forest Full of Rain* (Sono Nis); and 'A Sonnet Honouring Robin Skelton and His Muse on His Sixtieth Birthday' by Joe Rosenblatt in *Exile*. Florence Vale's drawing 'The French Girl' courtesy of Bram and Lynn Verhoeff.

Front cover is after a photograph by Susan Musgrave titled 'Robin Changing Film at Lanyon Quoit, Cornwall, 1970'. Back cover is a photograph of Robin Skelton by Marcia McNeill Willis.

Typeset in Sabon by The Coach House Press (Toronto). Printed on Zephyr Antique laid, sewn into signatures and bound by the Porcupine's Quill, Inc.

ISBN 0-88984-092-X

Contents

Introduction

FOR SOMEONE GROWING UP in Victoria BC in the 1960s, it was hard to avoid meeting Robin Skelton. It seemed as if wherever you looked, there he was: declaiming poetry in public lecture-rooms, introducing visiting artists, exhibiting in galleries, browsing in junkshops, watching his plays performed. He even had a column in the *Victoria Daily Times*. My mother, who knew him socially, raved about his charm and talent. My older sister eulogized his lectures at the university. For all these reasons, and especially the last two, I had given him top billing on my long teenage list of People to Avoid. I just knew I wouldn't like him.

Somehow, despite few close calls, I managed to escape Victoria with my resolve intact. But I was amazed to find that the problem did not end there. In college seminars and on notice-boards three thousand miles from home, his name kept popping up like a bad penny: he was reading; he was lecturing; he was on his way. And no sooner had I settled in for my first drink at my first academic conference, in Toronto, when a classmate informed me, 'Robin Skelton's over at the bar. I told him you were from Victoria, and he thinks he knows your family.' 'I'm underage,' I announced, as if I'd just remembered it, 'I have to go now,' and I set down my drink, untouched, and scuttled for cover.

Had I *really* not met Robin Skelton? The further I got from Victoria, the more my answer seemed to astound people. On the west coast of Ireland or in the dank fens of Cambridgeshire, all I had to do was admit to being Canadian for the question to bounce back: 'Do you know Robin Skelton?' And frankly, the truth was beginning to surprise me too. It wasn't as if there was anything else going on in Victoria. When I looked back at those years, I began to wonder what I had been saving myself for.

Finally, on a spring night in Toronto, it happened. Or, more accurately, I made it happen. The 'Night of One Hundred Authors', a $250-a-plate dinner staged by the Writers' Development Trust, was underway, and I was eating mine on behalf of *The Financial Post*. When the meal was over and people had begun to circulate, I noticed Robin, standing alone with his back against a wall and looking oddly uncomfortable. All right, I told myself, say hello.

'Hello,' I said. 'Are you Robin Skelton? I think you were a friend of my mother's.' When I told him her name he perked up, pulled me toward him, and for a moment it was like being hauled onto the cowcatcher of a locomotive – the looming black hulk, a flash of silver, and the familiar 'Chuff, chuff, chuff' of the engine starting up.

'Ah yes,' he told me, beaming. 'She and I are great friends. And how *is* your mother? What's she doing?' Then I knew how it feels to be barrelling down the tracks at full steam, the only person aboard who knows the bridge is out. There was nothing to tell him but the truth.

'Oh, you mean my mother? She's – well, actually she's been dead for the past eight years.'

It wasn't until I'd come to know Robin and his family much better that I began to realize what gaps in time and space his friendships can in fact span. Friendships with people who had known for decades what I was just finding out: that in addition to being a writer of the first rank, Robin Skelton is the best of companions – frank, spontaneous and, perhaps because he is so prolific in his own right, unusually generous in his regard for other people and their work. There could not be less about him of the Great Man I had been trying for so long to avoid.

Even so, I was unprepared for the avalanche of enthusiasm that greeted my requests for contributions to celebrate his sixtieth birthday. 'What a lovely idea!' was the recurring refrain, 'I'm so glad to see my old friend honoured in this way.' No matter how long it had been since they last met, the bond was firm: 'Love and good wishes to Robin. *Tell him this,*' G. Wilson Knight wrote in red on the back of his envelope, forty years after the fact and only four days before his own death. Even those who, like British poet and scholar Kathleen Raine, said they disliked the idea of a Festschrift, made an exception of this one, both for friendship's sake and because, as she put it, 'He has done much to give Canada a literary identity.'

Certainly, there is much to dislike in traditional *Festschriften* – a clutch of academic essays, disinterred from the bottom drawer to speed the parting of an 'esteemed colleague', or else a grave panegyric, as unstinting as it is unlikely. But it was obvious from the outset that this volume could never be either of those things. Few of Robin's friends have had the time to write unpublishable essays: they are poets, painters, novelists, actors and publishers first, and academics second, if at all. And as for hagiography, clearly they know him all too well for that.

The resulting celebration is, by customary standards, an unusual one. It combines fiction, poetry, anecdotes and essays with photographs, collages and paintings – all of which claim Skelton as their subject, object or inspiration. In addition to their own intrinsic interest, these tributes serve a biographical function: for those already familiar with his poetry, they provide a rich background of commentary on the life behind the poems. To further that function, I have arranged the contributions with reference, where possible, to chronology, and appended a brief factual outline of Skelton's life as well as a complete bibliographical checklist, for reference. Finally, the book also affords, for the first time, a close look at some of Skelton's 'work in progress' – work which suggests that at sixty, he is only now reaching the height of his creative potential.

The portrait of Robin Skelton that emerges here, at the hands of sixty friends, is funny, respectful, wry and even scurrilous by turns, frequently self-contradictory and always loving – in short, a fitting likeness of the man himself. It is still, I would maintain, a Festschrift, but festival writing of a new and different kind: writing that celebrates both accomplishment and friendship, in a festival suitably grounded in the magic of the earth.

SIXTY

I take it easy here,
 as who does not?
It is the place for it
 and I have come
 to understand that I
 must take my place
 among the small
 contentments, comprehend
 the gentler, subtler
 messages of time
 that each succeeding day
 persuade my ear
 a little more distinctly
 in the way
 that long discarded
 languages grow clear
 with casual daily use.
Once, I am sure,
 I was word perfect
 but I don't know when
 unless it was - -
 but you would think me odd
 were I to hint at that,
 so I'll suppose
 it only is the mind,
 the ageing mind,
 that thinks it knows
 the roads on which it goes.

ROBIN SKELTON — Scripsit Sylvia Skelton.

Portrait of Robin and Sylvia Skelton, acrylic 1984 by Myfanwy Pavelic.

'Poetry creates the poet, and not vice versa.' RS

G.R. *Wilson Knight*
Memoir

ROBIN SKELTON was a leading student in the English Literature
Department during his time at Leeds. Besides his work in the
honours course his contribution was striking on the periphery of
English studies. Himself a poet of stature, he gave impetus to
others: his influence was strong in early association – if I
remember correctly – with the departmental anthologies, *Leeds
University Poetry*. His support of the Leeds University Union
Theatre Group was also valuable; his comments on my own
productions and acting were among the most astute that I have
had.

Again, in Canada, he has pursued a similar course with still
greater effect. *The Malahat Review*, of which he was the original
stimulus and first editor, has become an outstanding journal of
poetry and the arts, radiating its appeal across the western world.

Today he can look back on an achievement not only firm in
itself but also in its influence on the artistic community.

Alex Currie
Advice for Sloth

Do not look ahead into the day;
this night of now with its deep pulses beat
is adequate for all you have to say:
lie close beneath the warm accepting sheet.

THIS IS THE FIRST VERSE of the first poem in the first volume of the published corpus of Robin Skelton's poetry. The poem is 'Advice from Sloth' and it appears in *Patmos and Other Poems* (1955). There may be commentators who will elucidate its literary qualities and place it in a study of the development of the Skeltonian style. It is my friendly, affectionate duty in this sixtieth birthday tribute merely to confirm that, at the time these first poems were being written, it was indeed difficult to get Robin up in the morning. I know, because I used to try.

During the early 1950s we shared a flat in Manchester, both being young members of staff at the university; I was in the administration and Robin was in the English department. It was a time of great joy and potential with lots of marvellous talk, wit and good fellowship. The flat in a very respectable Manchester suburb was presided over by Mrs. Jones, a fondly remembered lady who, with her husband, balanced an ingrained pride in her home with a warm regard for the successive young gentlemen from the university who so often came within an ace of wrecking it. She had one endearing trait – at least it seems endearing in retrospect: she could lay paint on any surface faster and more unexpectedly than anyone Robin and I had ever met. She was the fastest brush in South Manchester. On returning to the flat late at night and in the dark it was advisable to pause in the hall, adjacent to the bedroom of the lightly-sleeping Mrs. Jones and her snoring spouse, to have a few sniffs to try to detect what particular sections of the wall, floor and banisters had been painted since we left the house a few hours before. The railings on the stairs were in a constant state of varnished tackiness and it was commonplace for razor blades on my mantlepiece to be painted into a perpetual immobility, like flies in amber, while I was out.

To return to my theme: late nights led to early mornings and the need for Robin to get to nine o'clock lectures and for me to begin my busy committee schedule. 'The dawn' – indeed – 'steals every private world away,' or as Harry Lauder used to sing, 'Oh its nice to get up in the mornin', but it's nicer to stay in bed.' That quotation brings in the other part of this convoluted story. I am a Scot: that is I belong to a race which is good at pretty well everything – especially boasting – and it will come as no surprise to hear that I make a superb plate of porridge. Robin, like all others, had fallen under its spell and many a plate we consumed of an evening while he read me his latest poetical efforts and we discussed university affairs. The stuff I made was thick, smooth, scalding hot, salted, not (under any circumstances) sugared, and, – although I say so myself – irresistible. It became for me – and, as this story will reveal, for Robin also – an antidote to Morpheus, my 'Advice for Sloth'.

I had soon realized that Robin did not care to bound out of bed at the first rumble of Phoebus' chariot (as they used to say in South Manchester) and I spent a number of unhappy mornings trying to cajole him to get up. Threats of professors of English standing with their watches at the ready by the lecture room door; whispers that Mrs. Jones was creeping upstairs with a loaded brush in each hand to paint the blankets; shouts from the landlord that in his day folk that slept in after five o'clock in the morning were horsewhipped; all those led to nothing. Occasional grunts and unconvincing comments to the effect that a poem was being composed were the only response. Then it came to me: my stroke of genius that would get his feet on the floor. I made the porridge in the morning. I took a plate of it, steaming hot, afloat with creamy milk, veritable *grand cru classé,* through to Robin's bedroom and set it on a table to the windward side of his bed *without a spoon.*

Now, as Jane Austen might have remarked, 'It is a truth universally acknowledged that a single poet (or anybody else for that matter) cannot eat delicious, tempting, scalding porridge without a spoon,' so I retired to my room and proceeded to demolish with noisy satisfaction my plate of blissful temptation – and I waited. It worked like magic (and Robin was always interested in that). I detected stirrings, then a wheedling voice; I knew what it was going to say (after all this time I had written the script). 'Alex, you've forgotten the spoon.' All that was required on my part was a brisk whistling, a clatter of plates and a studied disregard of the request. The anxiety rose in the voice and there were signs of panic from the bedroom. 'Alex, Alex – a spoon – a spoon!' 'Steady, Black Watch!' I hissed to myself and said never a word to the poor tormented man. At last, aware that the porridge was cooling and losing its tongue-burning splendour, Robin was up in a flash, leaping along the landing and into the kitchen drawer for a spoon. Success: as he fell on the porridge it became obvious that maybe the day wasn't going to be so bad after all; maybe it would be just as well to stay vertical for an hour or two and get to the university on time; maybe there was a world to win 'out of' Eden!

Well, as they say, the rest is history: a small plate of porridge, maybe, but a tidy enough leap for academe and literature. Where indeed would Canada be without the Scots?

Two small points to finish: Robin's poem includes these lines:

> The light exposes every dreams decay,
> presents accounts we cannot hope to pay.

They remind me he never did pay me for all that porridge.

Second, the landlady's husband, George, was a great character in his own right and Robin and I shared some memorable evenings with him – but I'll leave their recollection, with my continuing love and admiration, for the Seventieth Birthday Celebrations.

Michael Seward Snow
The Peterloo Group

MANCHESTER in the late fifties was certainly not without culture. It had good libraries, good theatre, an excellent orchestra, and one of the world's finest collections from ancient Egyptian cultures, all sustained by the city's Victorian heritage of industrial greatness and the philanthropy that accompanied it. But at that time Manchester seemed, on the whole, happiest with memories of the hierarchic Egyptian and Victorian societies, bristling with similar imperial values and similarly stolid. These Egyptians and Victorians were after all so respectable, so safely dead, and an attachment to them was unlikely to involve one in the discords of contemporary life. A small number of sympathetic citizens had striven for years to encourage an awareness of contemporary arts, but any young writers or artists had, for the most part, to show themselves in London rather than in Manchester. The affection for tranquil stasis was so marked that I remember an art historian responding to the invitation to view my studio, 'No thank you, I'm not interested in living artists, only dead ones'!

It needed a fair mixture of youthful idealism and concern, perhaps not totally untouched by arrogance, for three of Manchester's living artists to resolve to alter that situation, still more to name ourselves 'The Peterloo Group'. The word 'Peterloo' has had crusading and radical associations in Manchester ever since the 'Peterloo Massacre' of 1819, when a peaceful meeting of some sixty thousand unarmed people demanding Parliamentary reform was broken up by the nervous authorities, with the loss of a dozen lives and many hundreds injured. We hardly ran the risk of being shot, though there were plenty of individuals with vested interests ready to shoot us down in the other sense. But all three of us were convinced that for artists forced to work on their own for years with almost nothing in terms of audience, creative criticism or moral support, there was the threat of another sort of death – the danger that they would simply give up, eventually, in isolation. It was to provide such support that 'The Peterloo Group' came into being.

I imagine that Robin Skelton had been appointed to a lectureship in Manchester University on the basis of his academic skill. I think it seemed, to him at least, as though the fact that he wrote poetry, and even attracted critical acclaim for it, was something that the institution tolerated rather than wanted. Like

Plato, the university was perhaps aware of the necessity to exclude the creative artist from the ideal city, aware that is, of the uncomfortable effects that such people are liable to produce upon orthodoxies of any kind. How, after all, was one to arrive at a 'correct' critical view if the poet was not only not dead, but liable to produce additional work that might render one's assessments instantly out of date! And if it was impossible to have a correct critical view of the total context, one could only respond on a basis of personal sensitivity and imagination – an unduly subjective intrusion upon the search for proper academic objectivity.

Tony Connor had lived all his life in Manchester, earned his living as a designer and was happily aware that artists and poets were ultimately people, not unlike himself, who happened to be painting pictures and writing poems out of their own rich perceptions. I myself, though born in the city, had seldom lived there and had recently spent some years as a professional artist in Cornwall and come to be part of what was then the only professional group of artists in England working outside the influence of London.

Our programme was well thought out, so thought out that we could see our only hope of success was not to have one. To espouse any particular platform was not our aim, but rather to find and sustain those other people, like ourselves, struggling to carry on in a somewhat frosty environment. We wanted no adherents, no politics, no actual 'group' indeed, beyond the three of us. All we promised was to meet in a pub once a month, prepared to demonstrate and discuss our own work with one another and with anyone else who cared enough about such things to take part and share their work and their enthusiasms with us. We did aim to overthrow barriers to the appreciation of contemporary work, but to do this from the inside by sharing the common working experiences, and speaking always from the standpoint of creators. Everything could be questioned. Guests were encouraged to bring their own efforts instead of merely being passive spectators of a cultural sport.

Having distributed our manifesto, we were in some doubt as to whether anybody would come to the first meeting. In the event, a large number turned up and were kind enough to give us a hearing. Meeting in a pub helped a lot. Many shy participants felt better after a drink, and I remember singularly little violence other than the verbal kind. That, there was plenty of. Guests were often puzzled and affronted by the work produced and, as is usual in such circumstances, found that the best defence for their troubled sensibilities was to attack the work that challenged them. All this was taken in good part and the audience was often outspoken in our defence too. As meeting followed meeting it became clear that such a set-up was far more useful for the poets and writers than it could be for the painters and sculptors, who were, in any case, much in the minority. The opportunities for quiet contemplation of a painting were better provided by the exhibitions that were subsequently organized elsewhere, but the long-running battles between more representational and less representational painters remained a reliable fuse with which to touch off a passionate argument.

Some friends were disappointed that we apparently had no politics, that we were unprepared to tie the evolution of contemporary art to the proffered banners of the left or right. Others again were denied the solace of our exclusive support for their particular artistic orthodoxy – the supremacy of Renaissance Art, the Symbolist Movement, whatever it might be. Everyone was assured of a hearing, but equally everyone had to bear the reactions of the audience. Some felt that quieter voices would not be heard in such a mêlée. They underestimated the audience, and I remember the silence and respect with which the complex, poetic patterns of some of our most experienced associates were received.

Paying for the room was simple. We passed a hat round. It was also passed round on more than one occasion to provide a little financial and moral support for one of the finest poets of the English language known to us, who happened to be desperately poor at the time.

The excitement generated produced more creative activity. People who had apparently had no audience at all for their work now had at least the group to listen to them. People were not only put into touch with one another, they were put into touch with themselves. The effects of this were not always simple and were indeed quite impossible to predict. The release of a creative personality previously kept decorously in check had social consequences too. One knew that some associates began to have professional successes with their pictures, plays, and poems. It was also true that some lives were changed, careers evolved, relationships revised and a certain amount of divine discontent generated. But my happiest image is of two friends in the midst of such animated conversation when the pub emptied us all out, that they wandered off into the night, continued their argument in a convenient railway carriage, and woke the next morning, two hundred miles away in strange town!

After two or three years it became impossible for us to continue as a triumvirate. I had to live elsewhere and the pressures of other work made it difficult for my companions to operate in quite the same way. Such was the impetus of the larger group however, that long after we had officially announced the conclusion of 'The Peterloo Group' as such, its supporters continued to meet.

'The Peterloo Group' had no funds, no grants or scholarships to distribute. Its very success demonstrates to me that, although these things are vitally important, there yet remains a type of 'support for the arts' which is even more necessary to the survival of the creative artist. Poets and painters do not ask society for a blank cheque. They need our involvement and personal interest: the assurance that, win or lose, their exploration of our human boundaries is something that enlarges our awareness of ourselves and of human community and is therefore essential to our full development as people. It is my experience that programmes intended to be supportive of the arts can all too often fail to stress this simple fact. The arts do not exist simply to decorate, to function as a polite gloss upon the ugly struggle for human survival. If they were to be of interest merely to the dilettanti, the speculators or the snobs, they would not merit the support all thoughtful and sensitive people recognize they deserve. I believe that it is always useful to discriminate amongst the ways in which we finance the arts – to discriminate, that is, between those funds which are needed for the presentation of art and those which are of even more fundamental support because they help artists and writers and composers to actually produce more art. 'The Peterloo Group' did apply their energies to this latter problem and more work, much of it good, was in fact produced as a result. The experiment consequently remains relevant today because the need for informed enthusiasm is certainly no less. Given the presence of the right people in the right place, 'Peterloo' cost very little in terms of money but a great deal in terms of creative, individual energy.

Robin Skelton has always been rich in this sort of energy and he played a crucial part in 'Peterloo', both in generating the initial enthusiasm in a way which overcame people's natural diffidence and in sustaining, with infinite patience and understanding, those many creative spirits who knew the limitations of their own poetic achievement, but still aspired to reach out beyond them. This he managed to do without ever exhorting them towards a particular mode of expression, a particular artistic cabal, but always by his belief in their individual potential and his respect for their individual worth as people. Such guides and teachers are all too rare and such an achievement comes only to those with wide artistic experience, technical competence and generosity of spirit. Many meetings of the Group were illuminated, not simply by his poems but by his readiness to share his own working process and thereby encourage others to share theirs. He has always known that artists must help one another and that there are always more of them about than one at first suspects. It has always been clear to him that the arts have a health-giving and thoroughly functional role in human society and his work for 'The Peterloo Group' was one of the many ways in which he has consistently put his belief into practice through the years.

Tony Connor
Child and Man

Here is a snapshot of me —
twine-toed, doubtful, one year old —
throwing a ball at a gate.
Any infant, it could be:
I can't think of that large-skulled
creature as my intimate.

And yet I must, I suppose:
an unbroken thread of thoughts,
feelings, dreams and what-have-you,
leads from big head and twine-toes
to the professor who sits
here with new glasses askew.

I study him in the black
window across my workdesk;
he peers at me from the night,
as though to say: 'Now this tack
brings no gain, and puts at risk
the poem you wish to write.'

Well, I don't know about that;
but the little chap's no chance
against my shadowy twin,
who specializes in flat
denials, and good hard sense,
when dealing with reckless kin.

Best draw the curtains — shut out
his face, and middle-aged cant.
He likes aborting new things,
while I play on through my doubt,
as dead-set as this infant
on what the next second brings.

Geoffrey Holloway
Begging the Dialect: Attingham Park 1960

IT WAS IN 1960 that I first met Robin. The Third Programme had commissioned him to do a series of talks on modern poetry; these were to be followed up by a weekend at a Further Educational Centre. The one chosen was Attingham Park.

Attingham Park, the property of Sir George and Lady Trevelyan, was a great house in its own grounds, cool, with expansive balconies, a curling stream, and a mobile mist that when one got close enough resolved into deer, spectral, with frost-flower heads. You could walk barefoot on the lawns; indeed, the girls on the course did.

Almost, you could have said, an oasis. Very much so for me, since this was the first chance I'd had of meeting a writer of calibre. In those days, it should be remembered, there were few magazines, no poets in libraries, no Arvon courses during which one could hobnob with pros, picking up tips, short cuts into the way of poem-making. One felt isolated. Sometimes, even, that the impulse driving one to scratch soundmarks on paper was an idiot reflex, and that the people one heard of who apparently did the same were collectively screwy.

Anyway, here was Robin. He hadn't, then, evolved that combination of kilt-and-buzzard's nest that was to grace his chin in later years. Rather did he look like a Fortnum and Mason teddy bear that had been somehow mislaid by John Betjeman. He was with a friend of his, the painter Michael Snow. They had just returned from a foray into Cornwall and emerged with a gallery of six-foot colour photos. These they duly exhibited in the lecture room, partly to complement the poems of *Begging the Dialect,* which had come out that year, and a lot of which was set round Newlyn, with its 'fishbox houses'. Pictures, poems, of dolmens, Celtic crosses, tors, what have you.

What he did was read, natter, and chuckle, in the most companionable way imaginable. What we had there was, patently, an eclectic, an enthusiast, a patron, and a democrat. We heard about 'Tom' Blackburn and 'Jimmy' Kirkup, liberally larded with chunks of their work, about Edwin Brock the policeman poet (if he'd have been a rag and bone man Robin couldn't have been better pleased), and about John Knight, whose first book Robin had assiduously and delightedly promoted.

Also, about 'doing' books – apparently an activity only a little more complicated than making paper flowers. But – this was the great thing – completely natural. Another thing, that one could write about anything, in any way. As listening to the various, the virtuoso *Begging The Dialect* demonstrated. It was amazing, everything – so heartening it hurt.

One could of course go on endlessly about *Begging The Dialect*. Let me stay with a couple of poems, favourites. The one he started with, if I remember, was 'Message For My Father'. We listened, and we were home, all of us. An effortless thing effortlessly read – and, this was important to me, filial. I'd lost my father in the First World War, but I knew what was meant – anyway, I had a grandfather.

> I'm never certain what the message is
> except that it is quiet and in words.

Then this, of the apple tree in his father's garden:

> ... Transfigurations talked
> crowded as sparrows in its bitten leaves

and, clinchingly,

> Yet how am I to say ... what can't be said
> except by silence? I talk silence out
> until it comes back filled with every phrase
> of hesitation, every false start
> the passion, the inquiry, and the love.

As well as a personal tribute to someone loved, it could stand as an apology for the poetic process.

My other darling was the one from the 'Speech is Common' sequence, called 'A Ballad Of The Four Fishers'. Remarkable in that it wove together a root-archetype (in this case the sea- rather than the earth-mother), a dramatic monologue (it's the sea-mother that's the narrator), and a tragic, inevitable story that could have come out of nothing but the ballad tradition. Its other innovation was stanzaic; running two quatrains together gave each verse a massive, oracular quality. I say 'oracular' advisedly, since to feel anything like its true power one has to hear Robin's poetry read aloud. (When I typed that sentence initially I put 'bread aloud', to find I'd chanced on something that would epitomize the whole of his opus; it is essentially just that.)

Anyway, here it was, in all its swagger, the baroque ferocity of its images, the slam of its rhythms, the strength of its exhortation.

> I got four sons. They gave me all
> that flesh and blood could bear.
> The holy dust ran like a mouse
> below the churching door.
> Sands scuttled fast as winds blew up
> before He blessed each head;
> the name-words tasted in my mouth
> of the red salt of blood
>
> Roust out your prayers and mercies now
> to tailor words for grief;
> I split the word jammed in my jaws
> with time's scaled gutting knife.
> I lay my child-torn belly on
> the friday of the stone;
> the elder clasps his cockle hands
> and all my grace is done.
>
> I had four sons across my bed
> below the weed-green wall;
> under the hunting of the gulls
> you'll hear their voices call,
> and one and one and one again
> they sweep across my eye:
> blind hands reach to the blinding sea
> and my grey belly dry.

25

I listened, and I thought I don't care what else he's written, or going to write, this is it. IT. And he knew it too, the old so-and-so. I hope he still does.

Robin Skelton reading Yeats at The Lantern Theatre, Dublin 1965.

Liam Miller
Robin Skelton and the Dolmen Press

THIRTY-FOUR YEARS AGO, when my wife Jo and I set up a tiny
handpress in our Dublin home to print and issue the work of new
Irish poets, we could never have predicted that the Dolmen Press
imprint would still be carrying on that work in 1985. The
handpress is long gone, as are the 'trade' letterpress and printing
shop that succeeded it – sacrificial victims of offset, computers,
and 'progress'. But our most treasured mementos of those early
years are still with us: the friendships extended to us through our
small enterprise.

It was the publication of Thomas Kinsella's first major
collection of poems, *Another September*, that first brought Robin
Skelton to us. He was in Dublin, researching the manuscripts of
J.M. Synge for his four-volume Oxford edition, and had occasion
to review a copy of our book for *The Manchester Guardian*. Our
parallel enthusiasms and obsessions – poetry and Synge and
theatre and printing and Sturge Moore and Bottomley – formed an
immediate bond, and Robin's benevolent interest in the Dolmen
Press was instant and enduring.

Perhaps Robin's greatest contribution to the survival and
development of the Dolmen Press was persuading John Bell, his
editor at the Oxford University Press, to take a general look at our
work. After a number of meetings, we reached an agreement
whereby Oxford would become general distributors of our books
outside Ireland. (Thus, for example, Austin Clarke's *Later Poems*,
the first Dolmen book issued under the agreement, achieved
worldwide notice and reclaimed Clarke's international reputation
in poetry.) This arrangement lasted for the next fifteen years,
creating for us an audience outside Ireland which we would never
have otherwise reached.

In 1959, to mark the fiftieth anniversary of Synge's death, the
Dolmen Press had planned to print an edition of his *Poems and
Translations* as originally printed at the Cuala Press in 1909, but
with colour lithographs by Tate Adams. One hundred and fifty
copies in Imperial octavo were the planned edition, to be handset
in Victor Hammer's American Uncial. In the end, the book did not
appear, but Robin saw our draft announcement and, as a result,
offered to help us produce a first edition Synge which he would
edit for us. This became *Translations*, for which he negotiated the
permissions of Mrs. Lilo Stephens, the Synge estate, and

Oxford University Press. The book was the second issued in conjunction with Oxford University Press and it included seven translations by Synge, printed for the first time, with an introduction by Robin.

Translations was the first of three Synge editions which Robin edited for us, and they are among the books of which I am most proud. Of the typefaces offered, Robin wrote that he preferred Centaur for *Translations*: 'it's got more of a carved simplicity.' The book was published in August of 1961, in an edition of seven hundred and fifty copies, Royal octavo, printed in black and red throughout, bound in blue boards with a vellum spine, and slipcased.

Our next Synge title was *Riders to the Sea,* edited from the manuscript in the Houghton Library at Harvard. Tate Adams, who had planned the lithographs for the never-issued *Poems and Translations* of 1959, provided five four-colour cuts for this volume, each of which had to pass through the press four times. This prompted a typographical experiment. We set the whole text of the book in one size (fourteen point Roman) of Gill's Pilgrim type and used colour to distinguish stage directions (grey), characters' names (red) and titling (blue). This meant achieving a fine register not only in the illustrations, but between as many as three colours in one line of text! *Riders to the Sea,* seven hundred and fifty Imperial octavo copies in buckram, appeared in August 1969, introduced by Robin's important essay on the manuscripts of the play.

In 1971, to mark the Synge Centenary, Robin edited and contributed an extensive essay to Dolmen's issue of Synge's translations from Petrarch, *Some Sonnets from 'Laura in Death'*. There, Synge's versions are printed facing the original Italian texts, and included are two portraits of Synge and Petrarch by Jack Coughlin. The standard edition consisted of six hundred and seventy-five copies in boards, but there was a special signed edition of seventy-five copies in full limp vellum, with two original drypoint etchings of the Coughlin portraits.

Also for the Synge Centenary, we published Robin's long poem, *Remembering Synge,* in our Poetry Ireland Editions. This was the third book of poetry from Robin's pen which we issued. The first, in 1964, was *An Irish Gathering,* a little collection which for me reflects Robin's early visits to Dublin and our wanderings about the city, sharing plans and hopes. A visit to the old quarter of the city, the Brazen Head Hotel, Saint Michan's in Church Street and the city walls, prompted his poem, 'At Emmet's Grave', which he dedicated to me.

Robin's second collection from our press is *An Irish Album,* published in 1969, which contains some versions of old Irish poems as well as his own observations of the Ireland he had grown to know better and, for all its failings, to love the more. He read his Irish poems to an appreciative audience at the little Lantern Theatre in Merrion Square in a season of poetry readings which also included Padraic Colum, Patrick Kavanagh and many younger Irish poets.

In a foreword written when *An Irish Gathering* was planned, Robin reveals the background to his love of things Irish, and I hope I will be forgiven for quoting a little unpublished Skelton here:

A Yorkshireman with a Welsh Grandmother can hardly describe himself as an Irish poet, and it is with some diffidence that I present this sequence of poems about Anna Livia, Dublin, and the Dead, for my history is not their history, and if I am moved I am moved by a story rather than by anything out of my own past or the past of my race. And yet, perhaps, this story is as much a part of me as it is of any born Irishman, for England and Ireland have been involved with one another in a love-hate relationship now for more centuries than it is easy to reckon up, and, as a poet, I am heir to the Anglo-Irish tradition of Congreve, Swift, Goldsmith, Wilde, Yeats, and Joyce equally with any Dubliner. I am also, of course, heir to much bloody history, much brutality, treachery and oppression. Maybe it is this that makes me turn my mind to Irish Themes, playing the part of a man expiating the sins of the past, indulging in a confession of history? Or perhaps it is, less romantically, that in Dublin I have a sense of something almost approaching a City-State, and one with its past still standing solidly about its present. This is, to an inhabitant of the Industrial North of England, a strange and moving phenomenon. It may be even that Dublin's Heroic Age could be said to be within living memory, and that there is a kind of headiness in walking the streets with men who played a part in the creation of a Nation. Perhaps, and more probably, it is that the stout is creamier and the hospitality warmer than in anywhere else I know.

Five years later, in *An Irish Album*, he explored that preoccupation in poetry, and for me this excerpt from 'For Dublin With Love' summarizes perfectly Robin Skelton's long love affair with Ireland:

> The formidable Uncles
> brought me into her house,
> and in sonorous tones
> said something inappropriate;
> on the wall
> was a photograph of Maud Gonne
> with a boss-eyed hound,
>
> and a purple Paul Henry landscape.
> I looked. I listened.
> ....
> And a black-bearded printer
> piled sugarlumps into a dolmen
> from which sweetness dropped,
> drip by drip, on the upturned mouths
> of sixteen poets, seven playwrights.
> and forty-five scholars
> engaged in outlining the final,
> the ultimate truth
>
> about Synge, about Yeats, about Swift,
> about Tara, commenting
> in between drips
> on the terrible state of the nation.
> I looked and I listened.
> And then one remarkable Uncle
> led me outback to the stars
> that filled the spaces
>
> between the grey decorous squares
> and I heard a singing.
> The words were no matter;
> they came clear and keen
> as a flute across lake water,
> as if the mountains
> around the city
> hunched to a secret tune

that no one could hear but the once.
I heard it, listened
to something still and chill
from the riot heart;
a blackbird under a hedgerow
might have known it,
or a curlew high on the moorland;
wilder than art,

and stranger than music,
it wandered like a woman
wandering, remote with love,
an unending garden,
impersonal in her possessing.
It soared, it fluttered,
delicate, vibrant, absurd
as the heart is absurd

always when touched or abandoned.
It was that moment
Ireland turned her head
and I caught the gleam,
stood there, ridiculous,
clumsy with alien language,
dropping my half eaten syllables
on the stones,

and wiping my mouth with a sleeve
that tasted of Guinness,
and feeling the wind round my heart.
Remote, absurd,
that sweetness lingered and lingers.
Back from exile,
I have made this poem
that the ghost may return.

Robin has never been appreciated enough for his promotion of
Irish poetry, beginning in 1962, when he edited *Six Irish Poets* for
Oxford University Press and presented to a wide audience a
generous sampling from Austin Clarke, Richard Kell, Thomas
Kinsella, John Montague, Richard Murphy and Richard Weber,
and continuing through his years as editor of *The Malahat Review*
in Victoria. Robin arranged a comprehensive exhibition of prints

for Victoria from the Graphic Studio in Dulin, and he persuaded
the library of the University of Victoria to collect Irish materials,
including major collections of material and books from the Cuala
and from our own press. He linked Cuala and the Dolmen in an
essay entitled, 'Twentieth Century Irish Literature and the Private
Press Tradition', in *The Massachusetts Review* in 1964. And in the
following year, to mark the centenary of W.B. Yeats, he was
largely responsible for the exhibition and symposium at Victoria,
'The World of W.B. Yeats', which was accompanied by a volume
of essays under the same name, edited with Ann Saddlemeyer. Due
to his efforts, visiting Irish poets and artists have become a regular
feature of Victoria's cultural life.

Inevitably over the years contacts have become fewer, not from
any wish that that be so, but from circumstances of time and
distance. Robin's visits to Ireland have been fewer of recent years,
but the enthusiasms which began in the late fifties still remain. I
am proud to add to this commemoration of one who has been a
significant figure in my own development.

John Montague
All Hail to Robin

ROBIN SKELTON first dropped into my basement flat in Herbert
Street, Dublin, in the early summer of 1960. He had his father-in-
law with him, a splendidly pugnacious trades union journalist
called Percy Jarrett, and that good poet from Salford, Tony
Connor. I presume they had all crossed over together on the
leisurely overnight Liverpool boat. And Liam Miller had pointed
the way over from the Dolmen Press in Upper Mount Street; the
press was then in its first blossoming fame.

As it happened I was working on my first book length
manuscript, *Poisoned Lands* (1961) and copies of key poems were
scattered across the table. There was also a good reserve of
Chateau St. James, bottled Guinness, to wash down or whet the
almost immediate cordiality between us. Robin was over to work
on Synge, and the great four-volume edition begins from that time,
but he was not only concerned with the great dead. The
enthusiasm with which he tackled some of those early poems,
'Like Dolmens round my Childhood' and 'Wild Sports of the
West', showed that he loved poetry with a passion that made light
of, mockingly ignored the traditional hostilities between Irish
bards and English literati. As we argued over or praised lines, it
became obvious that I had made a lifelong connection with
someone who really loved the Muse, and thought of poetry as a
glorious and shared adventure.

A year later, walking along Wicklow Street, he proposed the
anthology, *Six Irish Poets* (Oxford University Press) which was to
be a real breakthrough for my generation. Remember the Irish
writer's then inferior state compared to his English contemporary
in terms of opportunities: there might be *New Signatures,* or *New
Lines* or the Movement in England, but Irish poetry was an official
backwater with only the occasional conforming or performing
bogtrotter allowed in, as a gracious exception. Bertie Rodgers won
through the gift of the gab and Kinsella was in the second *New
Lines* anthology, but no one was really interested in us, except
visiting Americans, like Roethke. If that automatic colonialism has
changed a little, Skelton has been one of those who came to the
rescue.

Class, of course, was part of what linked us: he being directly
exposed to it in his daily professional life as an English academic;
the Irish, in a sense, being beyond and above it ('The indomitable

Irishry' boast of Yeats is true, in the sense that we do not, literally, give a fig about class if a man can sing a song or tell a tale or generally grace the company).

I saw Robin next, comfortable but uneasy in an English provincial university, generating warmth and generosity, but definitely a little too large for those surroundings. The learning grew, and the dedication to the art of poetry, but he lacked caution and seemed interested in everything – not just in a literary career based on the Oxford-London triangle. Another Yorkshireman he admired, Ted Hughes, could maintain his wary distance from the literati, but flat-footed Robin was no farmer. His erudition led him to the centre of the English tradition, Blake's Giant Forms, the symbols of Yeats, poetry as knowledge. In the era of Larkin, or the more spiteful Kingsley Amis, poetry was a sideline art, not a giant Vision of Albion or anywhere else, unless an arsehole.

All hail to Robin for having made the necessary leap out of that self-constricting atmosphere, the petty snobberies of English literary life. When we met next it was on his chosen island, at the other end of Canada. Hardly there than he was spreading the good news again, organizing *The Malahat Review*, and inviting guest speakers, including many wandering Irish scholars – Liam Miller of the Dolmen Press, Tom Kinsella, myself. Victoria would learn about the outside world, and the outside would hear of the strange resources of Vancouver Island. I read there twice and came back to stay for a term, my only regret being that I did not immerse myself enough in the low-lying but palpable mists of creative possibility that hung over the island, the strange post-Imperial grandeur of the Empress Hotel, the presence of the ocean and the mountains, the ubiquitous Indians. The best single creative workshop I have yet had was at the University of Victoria, and Robin's generous and organizing energy has made us aware of that Pacific Coast Twilight.

Robin and Sylvia also appeared at my little shieling in Paris, 11 Rue Daguerre, a few doors way from Hayter the engraver, and the solitary Beckett. But as always, Robin had his projects well in view: he helped to bring David Gascoigne back into print and, of course, he had his secret meetings with Zuk, in a cafe I suggested as being unknown to the literati: otherwise Beckett, Simone de Beauvoir, Sartre, Brassai and Giacometti, who were all neighbours, would have sought to join in the fun. 'Zuk Ahoy' was a password in those days and now that the first official non-biography is being prepared in Ispahan, the most closely guarded literary friendship of the Sixties is endangered.

Robin also revisited Dublin, in pursuit of the Muse, when I was back teaching at the old UCD. As always, we had many fine sessions, like working on the proofs of *Tides* with the publisher, Liam Miller, and a future illustrator, Jack Coughlin, in a hotel called The Majestic which has since disappeared. Robin was aware, like us all, that something strange and unpleasant was happening to the varied Dublin life he had first got to know in 1960: a vicious, creeping commercialism was pulling down noble streets, closing old-style restaurants and hotels, like Jammets and The Wicklow. And he was sharply aware of the limitations of that self-seeking, self-advertising subdivision of Irish literature known as Bluster Poetry.

So Robin Skelton was a generous presence in Irish letters for well over a decade, at a crucial time when we were moving away from, while respecting, the achievements of the first Irish Literary Renaissance. I am grateful to him for his literary comradeship on so many occasions; the last was in my own chosen exile in Cork where he, and Susan Musgrave, whose work he had shown to me years before, appeared as a Canadian double-bill which I called the Witch and the Wizard. One of the splendid things about Robin is that he has never been afraid of the mystical aspects of poetry but he allies it with profound feeling for the technical; his handbooks on poetry are among the few I would recommend to an apprentice poet. Poet, anthologist, editor, essayist, he has been a one-man band for so long that people tend to take his generosity and skill for granted. But I think he has had a salutary influence on both Irish and Canadian literature, as well as maintaining his central devotion to poetry itself. And finally there is his great sense of fun: the morning after that reading in Cork we went off to hear jazz, and then plunged into a pleasant party, before the Canadian convoy left for Galway. As Brendan Behan said about Paris, it was ever thus with Robin: some serious business, and then sport.
FLOREAT.

Thomas Kinsella
Robin Reigning as King Conchobor*

ULSTER GREW to worship Conchobor. So high was their regard for him that every man in Ulster that took a girl in marriage let her sleep the first night with Conchobor, so as to have him first in the family. There was no wiser being in the world. He never gave a judgement until it was ripe, for fear it might be wrong and the crops worsen. There was no harder warrior in the world, but because he was to produce a son they never let him near danger. Heroes and battle-veterans and brave champions went before him into every fight and fray, to keep him from harm. Any Ulsterman who gave him a bed for the night gave him his wife as well to sleep with.

His household was very handsome. He had three houses: Craebruad, the Red Branch; Téte Brec, the Twinkling Hoard; and Craebderg, the Ruddy Branch. The severed heads and spoils were kept in the Craebderg. The kings sat in the Craebruad, red being for royalty. All the javelins and shields and swords were kept in the Téte Brec; the place twinkled with the gold of sword-hilts and the gold and silver glimmering on the necks and coils of grey javelins, on shield-plates and shield-rims, and in the sets of goblets, cups and drinking-horns.

> Ochain was there, Conchobor's shield, the Ear of Beauty
> — it had four gold borders around it;
> Cúchulainn's black shield Dubán;
> Lámthapad — the swift to hand — belonging to Conall Cernach;
> Ochnech belonging to Flidais;
> Furbaide's red-gold Orderg;
> Cúscraid's triumphant sword Coscrach;
> death-dealing Echtach that belonged to Amargin;
> Condere's angry Ir;
> Nuadu's Cainnel — a bright torch;
> Fergus's hacking sword Leochain;
> the fearful Uathach that belonged to Dubthach;
> Errge's Lettach;
> Menn's Brattach;
> Noisiu's joyful Luithech;

*(from my translation of the Irish epic *The Táin*, part of a contributary story, the eighth century *Compert Conchoboir*)

Nithach the wounder belonging to Laegaire;
the bloody Croda of Cormac;
Sencha's resonant shield Sciatharglan;
Celtchar's Comla Catha, the Door of Battle;
and other shields beyond counting.   37

Also beyond counting were Conchobor's household and his
houses. There were one hundred and fifty inner rooms, each of
which held three couples. The houses and rooms were panelled
with red yew. In the centre of the house was Conchobor's own
room, guarded by screens of copper, with bars of silver and gold
birds on the screens, and precious jewels in the birds' heads for
eyes. Over Conchobor's head was a rod of silver with three apples
of gold, for keeping order over the throng. If it shook, or he raised
his voice, everyone fell into such a respectful silence you would
hear a needle drop to the floor.

Maurice Good
A Muse for Us (a crude collage)

Come, Muse, migrate from Greece and Ionia,
Cross out those immensely overpaid accounts, ...
Placard 'Removed' and 'To Let' on the rocks of your snowy Parnassus,
The same on the walls of your German, French and Spanish castles,
    and Italian collections;
For know a better, fresher, busier sphere, a wide
untried domain awaits, demands you.

THESE WORDS from that elemental American, Walt Whitman, have
always, for me, gloriously evoked Robin Skelton. At first, I wasn't
sure why. It has taken me some time to hammer it out. But,
'Would you care to write something for Robin's birthday?' was the
call, and instantly my fingers itched into action – poor
recompense, at best, for the heart's thrust. The job needs a poet, a
painter, or both, and I am neither. A flurry of facts jostle for
attention – and are mere facts to aid us? Still, a tentative portrait?
A crude collage?

Perhaps one of the more salient facts is that Robin Skelton, an
intrinsically unsettled character if ever there was one, is a
Canadian. Skelton's masks were made especially for cultural
tundras, for he is one of a kind, who travels with his muse forever
in tow. Such creative mechanisms as his are rare; as far as I know
he is unprecedented. When this golden-tongued and -boughed
Robin pulled up his earlier ancestral roots, they were to trail after
him like overland vines, instantly sending tap-roots into both
found and newly-cleaved fissures. A calculative as well as a
spontaneous phenomenon. Merely to think of him makes one
adventurous, and reach for *any* extravagant figure of speech.

But to return to the facts. It is a fact that Skelton is an
Englishman, born – that is, a fully-grown Yorkshireman, a pre-
natal poet, of ancient earth which delivers ripe fruit. Significantly,
however, he is also an honorary Irish poet, and was elevated thus
by the brotherhood of his peers among Hibernian bards. He's a
world authority on Anglo-Irish literature, and an Herculean
assessor of everything that matters most about it. He is also a full
professor, and a teacher of rare ilk. He was a founding editor of
The Malahat Review, to which the most gifted of global authors
clamour proudly and competitively in contribution. He's a critic,
too. But he's also a painter, sculptor, collagist, playwright,

dramaturg, short-story and mystery writer. Luckily for so many of the rest of us, he has even turned his attention to publishing.

Ah, but you can't stop there. He's a most lascivious bibliophile, saving his bacon sometimes as well as industriously bringing it home by auctioning off collections of already avidly thumbed tomes. And why not? There are always other tomes.... He's a crafty philatelist, and many like myself have enjoyed the full flood of his conversation while his seldom-resting fingers sift through the confetti of nations. This with a whole ear and sometimes an eye on family sit-coms. Yes, he is a husband and father, and yes, he really does watch television (with one eye), in light touch with our expiring twentieth century – detached yet sanguine participant. Notwithstanding our three generations of automobiles in the breakers' yards, Robin remains a dinosaur; never driving and always driven, he is a most determined pedestrian. Walkers, even among poets, are our rarest of breeds, but here is one such, a surviving link (via J.M. Synge) with Wordsworth and Coleridge. If you're looking (as I was once myself in younger and unhappier days) for an embodiment of the Renaissance man, here he is: a new, fully-fledged Medici of the West. And lastly, and more than anything else, and because he is indeed all of these things I've delighted to list, Robin is a warlock – a weaver of best spells, wielder of whitest magic.

It's fifteen years (or so) since I was introduced to Robin Skelton and we might never have met if we hadn't had the same publisher. Liam Miller of the Dolmen Press, demonic and saturnine (looking) catalyst, was to be the instigator of this lunch-time encounter in the stately surroundings of Yeats's old rooms in that quiet backwater of Woburn Place, London, West One. Neither Robin nor I had ever heard of the other. But we had both shared an unbridled love for, and immersion in, the works of John Millington Synge. My ignorance of the fact that Skelton was the undisputed world authority on Synge (he'd just finished editing the enormous, definitive Oxford edition of the collected works) was less explicable than his never having heard of *me*, a casual labourer in the arts and Anglo-Irish mummer who had finally (after years of *thinking* about it) grappled with Synge's works for eighteen months of absorbed wrestling and emerged with a one-man-show called 'John Synge Comes Next.' Liam Miller had been witness to its first performance at the Dublin Theatre Festival, its transfer to the Abbey Theatre, its televised and broadcast versions on the BBC, and had decided to publish it. For some years before, he'd been publishing Skelton's poetry and criticism.

When he summoned me to lunch with himself and Robin, he instructed me to arrive in character, if possible, with full moustache, big black hat, stout ashplant, and knapsack. Which is exactly what I did. When I strode in on them, Miller and Skelton were sitting at a small oval mahogany table crouched over large whiskies.

'Ah! *There* you are!' said Miller, waving a lean and elegant hand to me to join them, 'What'll you have?' And, turning to his amazed companion, he added, without pausing, 'Robin Skelton – meet John Synge.'

Robin's mouth, wide open in the great bearded face, was a chasm. For an instant, I took stock of this huge presence. I was facing a burlier, middle-aged Walt Whitman: wide-open-necked shirt displaying a chunky mandala framed by a pair of hieratic hangings on bare chest, disordered hair awry about a vast forehead. He looked as if he'd conjured up a long-awaited ghost. And in many ways, he had. A ghost which was to haunt him, often welcomed, sometimes admonished, though never – even after occasional attempts – quite absolutely exorcised.

Interspersed as it was between our initial exchange of explanations, greetings and courtesies, I soon became acquainted with, and enamoured of, the Skelton laugh: a conspiratorial indrawn cackle that – almost – beggars description. Tyrone Guthrie once described a certain actor to me as the only performer he'd known who could speak on an *intake* of breath. And Robin Skelton is the only actor (and I *do* mean actor) who can *laugh* in the same fashion: 'Cheuck – Cheuck – Cheuck – Cheuck' – each successive gleeful inhalation seeming to endanger its perpetrator with ultimate hyperventilation.

A bottle of wine (and more), a flood of talk, and some lunch later, the two of us, Skelton and Synge, had arranged a tryst for the following day. I was in need of a refresher rehearsal, a full run-through of 'John Synge Comes Next' as prelude to an impending British tour, and Robin had, he'd told me, a surprise of his own in store. I engaged a theatre for this special dress rehearsal at Berridge House (University of London), where I'd first rehearsed and previewed the show, and invited him to be its solitary witness. That rainy afternoon, the two of us the only occupants of stage and auditorium, was to change the course of my life.

We arrived by appointment at the theatre, and I left him sitting alone in the middle of empty seats, ruffling concentratedly (and a touch mysteriously) through some newly-typed pages, while I dressed and made up, after setting some lights and sound cues for the performance. 'John Synge Comes Next' was seldom played with such care or joy – except perhaps to two lone ladies who turned up once in Byblos to a cancelled matinée. Skelton watched and I worked. For a weird moment it reminded me of a scene in a western movie in which Judge Roy Bean booked out a whole theatre for himself to greedily savour the talents of Lily Langtry, Skelton being a fair double for Walter Brennan though myself hardly the Jersey. Now and then, towards the the end of part one and early in the second, I could hear the intaken cackle: 'Cheuck – Cheuck – Cheuck ...' When the show was over, and Synge had walked offstage into his stall of night, I returned to the stage to acknowledge the solitary applause of that delighted Robin.

Then, by previous arrangement, I took my place as audience while Robin Skelton ascended the stage to deliver a piece of his own: it was his first-ever performance of the long poem of homage, 'Remembering Synge'. From its first syllables:

> I move in his voice.
> Breath steams
> on the slow air
> of a grey dawn

I was transfixed. His shoulders were hunched over his pages (I'd provided him with a music-stand), but his look was lifted out front on every punctuation. The deep chest hurled the words forward, each one modulated, caressed, released into space through those gruff but lyrical tonalities. A deeply professional, because relaxed, performance, laced with restrained energy: a valuable lesson for anyone with the wit to learn from it. And, throughout the long, sustained text there was that encompassing sensation of Synge's own life, as much in the voice and performance as in the words, an astonishing evidence that Skelton and I had travelled the same journey to the same end.

Robin was approaching the close of his great poem:

> The heart of it is
> my waking here
> to the dark brothers
> the glancing girls,
> the ageless stories,
> a clenched fist
> of rock thrust
> at a wild sky.

Hard to tell if I was listening to Robin Skelton or to John Synge; the mystery of it was, of course, I was listening to both. It was a big trick, and a trick to which both our shows aspired. And, by the end of his reading:

> In him I remember
> strength gathering
>
> into a sign
> for the next journey.

I was aware, before their event, that there were journeys of my own to come.

On the way, since then and throughout my friendship with Robin, there's been a small measure of traditional backscratching. When my text of 'John Synge Comes Next' was published, my dedication was: 'To Robin Skelton – Who Knows Why'; on the appearance of his sumptuous Thames & Hudson biography, *J.M. Synge and His World,* his dedication 'To Maurice Good, whose stage portrait of J.M. Synge gives us the living man' was to be an encouraging crutch for me in a difficult year. But I'm prouder still of a more personal inscription which he made for me in his ceremonious scribe's hand. It's on the title page of his *Remembering Synge* (Dolmen Press), and I've no apology in quoting from some of it now as introduction to our following encounter: 'For Maurice Good, the first person ever to hear this poem read aloud, and one of its first readers ... on the memorable night of 'John Synge Comes Next', Victoria, Guy Fawkes Night, 1971.'

For of course it was Robin who saw to it that I made my first journey into Canada – though settling here, later was my own choice and invention. When he'd suggested that for the year of the Synge Centenary I could not do better than try a Canadian university tour and I'd protested that I'd no effective contacts nor little taste for grappling with academe, he'd bluntly asserted (his favourite saying), 'Why let a fact stand in the way.' He himself wrote the initial letters of introduction and promotion across the land, coast to coast, warning me that I'd have a deal of follow-through: 'And you'll do it, dammit! Mail, cable and telephone!' He warned me it might often be hard to pin down, frustrating and arduous: 'But in the event *tolerable,* man! They'll pay, they'll be lucky – and you're worth it!' Well, he was right: it was arduous, and it *was* worth it. After a farewell performance in Dublin I packed a big black suitcase (half Synge and half self) and flew into his continent. Earliest bookings on his doorstep – Victoria, Nanaimo, Vancouver – blossomed into a round dozen, sweeping me west to east: Calgary; Winnipeg (and forty below at Portage and Main); the trifiddic towers of York; calmer vistas of Queen's at Kingston or McGill at Montreal; an occasional respite with older friends such as Maurice Podbrey at Centaur and some adventurous nuns in White Plains, New York. Under direct Skelton tutelage I was learning fast, and it was under his roof I launched the first probes into a later trip to Beirut and a middle-east tour of 'Synge' before Arabs and Jews, between burst of their ongoing wars.

Being a guest in Robin's home, as I found on that first and later trips, could be an exhausting business. For it *was* a business, as I was to discover – an indoctrination into the deeper ploys of work-hustling: the niceties (and economy) of 'night-letters' rather than wasteful day-time cables, and long-distance telephone calls calculated for only the most judiciously selective moments; the newly-acquired mystique (for a staid European) of working-breakfasts close on the heels of late-night conversations with the alertest of Canadian poets, sculptors and painters. Many of those very personal recitals took us into exhilarated dawns, and dawns on Vancouver Island are strangely special – curiously long in coming, the light so belatedly and reluctantly creeping into that last edge of the western world. Harboured under Robin's roof, shelter then for a generous clutch (himself, wife Sylvia and three children, his mother, a very venerable St. Bernard, a covey of peripatetical cats), we found ourselves singing our way through to the earliest greetings of birds in the encroaching trees. Much of this earlier adventure (as with later ones) would be a total blur if I hadn't then adopted the habit of written notes at moments of relative stasis, too full-summed to set down here but invariably ending with another of Skelton's then-constant refrains: 'Stayed Up Late'.

I wonder if he still does? All his energies (as I hear by frequent report) remain constant. Some habits mellow, can, sensibly, be encouraged to diminish (one of mine being for so long a compulsion to telephone him midnight or noon from anywhere halfway round the globe). But I hunger more, being older myself and a touch more wise, for his real presence – as a man will through time and distance always long for his brothers. We had other encounters, times drawn over pole or Rockies for a working

gig or weekend chat and, at last, one truly sensible long-distance
call to him from Stratford, Ontario, to ask him to recommend a
possible publisher for my book, *Every Inch A Lear,* to which he
instantly laid claim, sight unseen, for his own Sono Nis Press. It

was as typical of myself that I was unaware, then, that he had
become a publisher, as it was typical of him to be certain that the
book would be worth his salt (and mine) and to set about printing
it between such stylish covers. But then it *is* style, as much as
anything, that makes this man. And energy. That sweat of the poet
that makes his ideal concrete. The last time I saw him, at one of
the cheapest and more tolerable of Toronto's hotels (tribal usage
forbids me to say where), his persona had blossomed from mid-
Whitman to mid-Tennyson. Not that he's really like either, though
the sum of both have a whisper of him. Not that images can
conjure him rightly, not this ever flowering into reality of a Robin
who migrates toward us and beyond us in any year.

I began with some of my favourite words from Whitman's
'Song of the Exposition', in which he invites the mother of muses
to abscond from older haunts and cleave to him in his newer
world. And Whitman concludes:

> I say I see, my friends, if you do not, the illustrious
> émigrée,
> (having it is true in her day, although the same,
> changed,
> journeyed considerable,)
> Making directly for this rendezvous, vigorously
> clearing a path for
> herself, striding through the confusion,
> Bluff'd not a bit by drain-pipe, gasometers, artificial
> fertilizers,
> Smiling and pleas'd with palpable intent to stay,
> She's here, install'd amid the kitchen ware!

As is Robin. Whitman's muse might sometimes be Skelton's. But
Robin, great invoker that he is, is as much to be found in his
special muse as that lady herself is always present for him. What I
now feel most about Robin is that he has become something of a
muse himself. Which is the main reason why we who labour in the
vineyards of the arts have always envied him a little, admired and
loved him. And I'm honoured, now, to be given this chance to
contribute to our celebration of these first six decades of such an
illustrious, maybe inexplicable, and constantly impudent, émigré.

Ink wash by Hilda Morris.

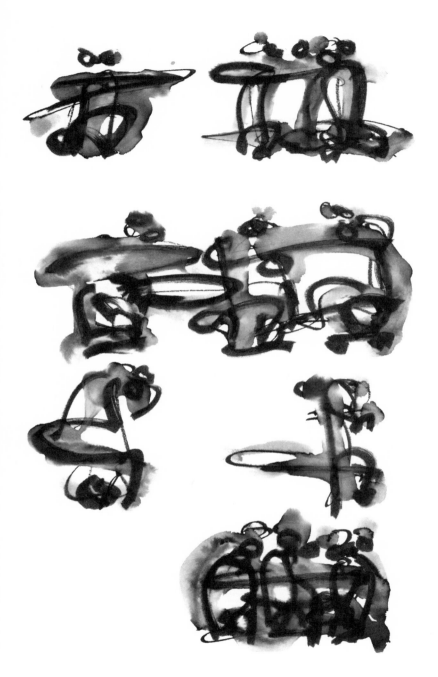

Watercolour by Carl Morris 1985.

George Cuomo
That Magnificent Mountain

ROBIN AND I BOTH started out as poets, some thousands of miles and one large ocean apart, although by the time we met in Victoria in the early 60s I was already beginning to think maybe I'd be better off sticking to something easier, like novels. Without meaning to, or even knowing he was doing it, Robin gave me the final nudge. Within a short period of time we both gave poetry readings. (It was a rare occasion indeed, as I pointed out in introducing Robin to his audience, having two poets on the same platform who together weighed over 400 pounds.) Both readings seemed to go quite well, and I was inordinately pleased, having more or less survived comparison with a poet as good as Robin Skelton. There was even some flattering talk that we should both give additional readings. That brought the hard truth home. Robin said he'd be delighted, and why shouldn't he have been? He'd just scratched the surface with his first reading; he had another dozen or so *books* full of poems, fine poems, terrific poems, as good or better than the ones he'd already presented. To say nothing of the poems he'd just written that month, or that week, or that day. So sure, he was raring to go. The man, I realized, was an inexhaustible resource. He thrived on poetry, it was his natural speech, his way of addressing himself and the world, his means of giving things shape and bringing the everyday fuzziness we all endure into some sort of focus. As for me, I'd given my all in a single shot. Those *were* my poems. And so, over the years since, they've remained my poems. I still sort of like a couple of them. So do a few other people. But they're like a rock in the road, solid enough, and maybe worth a glance. But there's a real mountain nearby, lovely and daring and awesome, that can take your breath away. It's worth exploring for hours, for days, worth coming back to again and again to appreciate the startling views, the unique formations, the permanence of its structure.

This is a salute to Robin, and that magnificent mountain.

George Hitchcock
How We Got From There To Here

Traffic lights turn red.
  Unsheathe your knife:
  The spotted wings of life
Drift overhead.

Fire has charred this sea:
  Here's where we turn,
  Halt, and relearn
The art of prophecy.

An ocelot appears
  Superbly tailored on
The off-ramp tiers
  Of the autobahn.

Please rewind and go
To passion's entrepôt.
  The lion shows its claws
  To mutual applause.

Approach the latter end
  And then reverse;
Kind hands may yet rescind
  The general curse.

George Woodcock
Admirable Eclecticism

THE 1960s WERE A particularly vital time in the development of a Canadian literature, not only in terms of the numbers of books and of new authors that were appearing, but also in the emergence for the first time of something near to the adequate structure of a literary world; Canadian-owned publishing houses, and magazines that were largely edited by writers, emerged in rapid succession and became the foci of regional as well as national literary movements, one of the most important of which was what Robin Skelton called, in a memorable special issue of *The Malahat Review* (Number 25) which he devoted to the subject, 'The West Coast Renaissance'.

One of the striking features of the West Coast Renaissance was the number of magazines of national and international scope which emerged in British Columbia during that period. The early 1950s had been a barren time for literary journals in the whole of Canada; on the west coast, *Contemporary Verse* – Alan Crawley's fine magazine of modern poetry, had closed down in 1952, and nothing had immediately appeared to replace it. The first move in re-establishing a Canadian network of literary magazines was made in Toronto, when Robert Weaver and his associates founded *Tamarack Review*, but the next three Canadian magazines of primary importance, all of them still flourishing, appeared in British Columbia: *Canadian Literature* and *Prism* in Vancouver in 1959, and *The Malahat Review* in Victoria in 1967.

Robin Skelton had arrived at the University of Victoria from England in 1963, and the novelist John Peter from South Africa at about the same time. They founded *The Malahat Review* together and shared the editing until 1971. Despite its very regional name, taken from the mountain one must cross driving northward from Victoria up Vancouver Island, it was intended from the beginning as an international magazine. And by 'international' Skelton and Peter meant something even more cosmopolitan in scope than the internationally respected magazines of the past like *Horizon* and *Partisan Review* in New York. In fact they were aiming at a journal even more international than earlier transatlantic magazines like *Transition*, which were largely devoted, whatever the nationalities of their contributors, to the encouragement and promotion of modernist writing in the English language. In fact, the only earlier journal I know that seriously attempted what *The*

Malahat Review set out to do was *New Writing* in its earlier period during the 1930s, when John Lehmann brought some important new European writers as well as new English writers to the attention of British writers and we read Silone's 'The Fox' between the same covers as Orwell's 'Shooting an Elephant'. But even Lehmann's effort was limited and marred by the fact that because of his political leanings he chose only left-wing writers at a time when, as Orwell shrewdly remarked, an amazing number of the best European writers were conservative or even reactionary in their politics.

51

Skelton and Peter rightly left political considerations out of their criteria; they also decided that *Malahat*'s originative role in the English-speaking world could only be assured if they published only material that had never appeared in the English language before, and this has meant throughout the long history of the journal – still appearing in its nineteenth year – that one has always opened the issues as they came with the certainty that whatever one sees will be new, and interesting for that reason to begin with, since even if the originals of foreign contributions have appeared elsewhere the translations have not.

I remember well the first issue in 1967, which admirably sustained the editors' international intent by publishing work by Robert Fitzgerald, Karl Krolow, Heinz Pointek and Rolando Tinio. It also established another excellent *Malahat* practice of publishing unfamiliar material relating to established writers by printing a group of John Betjeman's worksheets and a number of letters from D.H. Lawrence to Koteliansky.

Apart from my admiration for the task that Skelton and Peter had set themselves, and for the fine judgement with which they were obviously carrying it out, I felt a considerable sympathy for them since they were being subjected to the same kind of gloomy prophesies I had endured when I founded *Canadian Literature*. I had been told that I would soon run out of Canadian poets and novelists to write about and even if I found them, I would never recruit enough good critics to discuss their works. The great literary upsurge in Canada during the 1960s provided subjects and critics in abundance and confounded the prophets of doom. In the same way, Robin Skelton was told that he could not possibly succeed in producing an international journal from Victoria, of all places. Who on earth, with a chance of publishing in London or New York, would think of writing for him?

Besides, the orientation of *The Malahat Review* was resented on the one side by the American-oriented 'Tish' group which was emerging at this time in Vancouver and believed that the future of Canadian poetry was to be found in the American post-modern tradition and not in a cosmopolitan context, and on the other side by the Canadian nationalists who were temporarily in the ascendant and who xenophobically rejected both the idea of an international magazine and Skelton's English origins; they were further resentful that as a critic he had not paid due respect to the sacred cows – or more often sacred oxen – of Canadian literature, and had spoken his mind about the weaknesses of locally revered poets.

I have already begun to speak of *The Malahat Review* as if it were Robin Skelton's magazine, and in fact, long before John Peter's name vanished from the masthead in 1971 it was clear that Skelton was really running the journal and making all the important editorial decisions and most of the unimportant ones. Doubtless the situation was partly due to Peter's increasingly poor health, but it fitted in with the general history of magazine editing, which is rarely successful as a partnership. Out of two editors one will always take the lead and the other slowly drop away in importance, as happened in the partnership of Cyril Connolly and Stephen Spender with which *Horizon* started off; very soon Spender had ceased to be active and today we think of *Horizon* only as Connolly's magazine. In the same way the imprint of Skelton's taste and his concept of literature was dominant in *The Malahat Review* from the beginning, and, though at times there were editorial helpers, like Derk Wynand, Charles Lillard and William David Thomas, it remained his magazine until he finally handed over the editorship to Constance Rooke in 1982.

Skelton proved his original critics wrong on all counts. He obtained originals and translations of work by leading writers not only in western Europe and Latin America but also in Asia and in the Warsaw Pact countries, including Russia. Borges and Burgess, Akhmatova and Alberti, Theodore Roethke and Kathleen Raine, Krishna Rayan and Sakutaro Hagiwara, Atilla Joszef and Ferenz Juhasz, they were all there, and the very richness of the patterns they created gave the magazine a kind of verbal impasto that was reinforced by an excellent choice of illustrations – both photographs and reproductions of paintings and drawings.

But the great triumph of Skelton's editing, I suggest, was the way in which he created an international magazine that was also national and strongly regional. In fact, he did a great service to Canadian writers by selecting the best of their work and placing it beside the best work from abroad. In such a comparison the

Canadian writers, like Margaret Atwood and Irving Layton and Dorothy Livesay and many fine but less famous writers, did not suffer, and so Skelton helped to establish the maturity of Canadian literature and the fact that Canadian writers could hold their own in the company of writers from other English-speaking traditions (the English and American, Indian and Caribbean) and also of writers from quite different traditions. I was going to use the term 'alien traditions', but in fact one of the things Skelton proved triumphantly was that in literature, as in the arts in general, there is no alien tradition. Whatever our language, so long as we use it with skill and respect, we belong one to another.

The longer he stayed in British Columbia, the more Skelton became convinced of the presence on the west coast of a vital and distinctive regional tradition in writing and the other arts, and I think he was reinforced in this by the number of brilliant younger writers he encountered through the Creative Writing Department he founded at the University of Victoria. In his later years of editorship, more and more of these local writers found their way into the pages of *The Malahat Review* and had at least some hand in its editing. Finally, in a series of three large and splendid issues published in 1978, 1979 and 1981, Skelton celebrated 'The West Coast Renaissance' in all its aspects, devoting space not only to the work of the many living writers who have made British Columbia their home, but also printing translations of Coast Indian poetry and tales, and celebrating the many painters who have been one of the region's chief glories.

Special book-length issues devoted to specific authors or areas of literature have in fact appeared at intervals throughout *Malahat*'s history, sometimes edited by Skelton and occasionally by guest editors. They include *Herbert Read: A Memorial Symposium* (1969), which Methuen later reprinted as a book in England; *Friedrich Nietzsche: A Symposium to Mark the Centenary of the Publication of The Birth of Tragedy* (1972); *Gathering in Celebration of the 80th birthday of Robert Graves* (1975); *Austrian Writing Today* (1976) and *The Margaret Atwood Symposium* (1977).

In some of these special symposia, and in other issues, Skelton would print what one might call samples of literary archaeology – recently discovered manuscripts or letters from notable dead writers, like Lawrence and Richard Aldington, or from the youth of notable living writers, and this inclination to regard literature as a temporal continuum, and good writing as worth reading for the first time no matter when it was written, in a way reinforced the spatial continuum offered by *Malahat*'s international scope. This aspect of the magazine's policy was encouraged by another facet of Skelton's activity, for many of the items of this kind he published were drawn from the archives of British writers which, largely through Skelton's efforts, found their way to the library of the University of Victoria.

The Malahat Review under Skelton's direction was an example of editorial eclecticism at its best. It promoted no literary school in preference to another, and writers were considered not according to their political or prosodic theories, but according to the sheer quality of their writing. Skelton never made a fetish of novelty, and, indeed, the sense of tradition was strong in any reading one made of the journal. Yet there was no question of indiscriminate traditionalism; the tradition was clear and specific, that of modernism in its broadest sense. The continuity of that tradition was stressed, and what one often felt, reading unpublished material from fifty years ago beside newly written work, was the astonishing feeling of contemporaneity that is projected by the best writing of our century no matter what its year. To be published in *The Malahat Review* was to keep good and extraordinary company. One chose carefully one's offerings to Robin, and was proud when they appeared in his pages.

'A rare photograph of Robin Skelton as an art critic and
collector at an exhibition of Herbert Siebner "City-Scapes" in
1973 at the Provincial Museum, Victoria BC.' H.S.

'The Embrace,' collage, Robin Skelton.

Colin Graham
Skelton as Art Critic and Maker of Art

HAD THE CIRCUMSTANCES of his early life been different, Robin
Skelton might easily have become a painter. The signs were there
in childhood: he was constantly drawing and making little
sculptures. So lusty, even Gargantuan, is his appetite for visual
experience that his urge to create might well have found an outlet
through paint and canvas.

One is tempted to imagine him as a north-of-England Augustus
John, bearded, shaggy-maned, and with an inborn verbal facility
sufficient to have outshone John as one of the country's most
literate painters. Yet he would have differed from John in one key
respect. John was a conservative and not much given to stylistic
experiments; his occasional stabs at symbolism were on the whole
unsuccessful. Skelton's agile and adventurous mind, on the other
hand, would have made an easy conquest of the conceptual and
the symbolic, and would surely have taken him onto the ramparts
of the avant garde.

His collages give us a good idea of the kind of painter he would have
made, an artist who, perhaps like Miro, sought to combine the
techniques of surrealism with the structural rigours of late cubism.

It was in Baluchistan in 1946 that he first started using scissors
and knives to cut up illustrations and to paste them on a ground in
such a way as to create harmonious compositions. As an avocation
it seemed for a number of years to satisfy his need for visual
creativity. Dissatisfaction with what he was doing came only
toward the end of a couple of decades. He has summed up this
phase with the rather too severe remark that, 'My collages of the
fifties and early sixties were non-figurative and, predictably,
derivative, and after a time I found the majority of them extremely
boring. The patterns I was making were sometimes pleasing but,
on the whole, empty of meaning. They were no more than
decorations.' While some were indeed merely well-put-together
designs, others were more mysterious and hinted at meanings that
lay well below the surface.

The first public display of his collages took place in the late
1950s, when he showed in Manchester with 'The Peterloo Group'.
In 1966, three years after joining the English department of the
University of Victoria, he was persuaded to exhibit some of his
work at a small local gallery called Pandora's Box. 'The interest
they appeared to arouse,' he later wrote, 'sent me to work again,
and I exhibited fairly frequently during the rest of the decade, both

in jury shows of the Art Gallery of Greater Victoria and in a local gallery. By the time I had my second show, at Nita Forrest's Print Gallery in 1968, however, my style had changed. My work had become almost wholly figurative.'

During the next two years a trip to London, followed by travels around Europe, left little time for the making of paste-ups. When Skelton returned to Victoria he was invited to join a newly-formed group comprising a dozen of the city's leading artists. Of this group, which calls itself 'The Limners' and which includes such nationally and even internationally recognized names as Pat Martin Bates, Elza Mayhew, Myfanwy Pavelic, Carole Sabiston, and Herbert Siebner, he became the first vice-president. In the ensuing years he has, with few exceptions, exhibited only with 'The Limners'. This has by no means limited his exposure, for the group has shown in Calgary, Edmonton, Toronto, and the Maritimes, as well as in Victoria. As a result, his collages are to be found in public and private collections in Canada, the United Kingdom, and the USA. They have also appeared in publications as diverse as *Prism International, Jewish Dialog, Arts West, The Malahat Review,* and *Canadian Fiction Magazine.*

To describe the collages simply as the product of a literary mind would be quite wrong. It is deceptively easy to look at their strongly-charged symbolism and to conclude that their subject matter has been deliberately and knowingly put together by an intellect very much at home in the world of symbolics and Jungian depth psychology. Such assumptions are neatly undercut by the artist's own descriptions of their making. 'I do not think in words at all as I am composing collages. Whatever messages they present are a consequence of the images moving together under my eye as I clip, sort, and paste, worrying more about tone and composition than anything else.' One suspects that what is happening as he puts together these coloured bits of paper, and what accounts for the magnetic pull of the best of them, is that his subconscious mind is busily making free associations while drawing on its well-stocked memory of mankind's myths and symbols. That could explain why in his commentaries on these works he is able to suggest such vivid overt and covert meanings.

In 1983 the Porcupine's Quill in Ontario published a small book in which four dozen of the collages, reproduced in black and white, are analyzed by Skelton himself. These analyses he has described as, 'the commentary of a partially informed docent wandering around an exhibition by someone else.' In spite of this modest disclaimer, it is clear that he knows a good deal about what is going on inside the images. Take, for example, collage number 39, *The Embrace*. A bull is advancing down a dark forest path while nearby lovers embrace beneath a hovering bittern. Skelton suggests that, 'The bull is an obvious masculine image and the bird one of freedom. I think that the embrace is bringing a sense of freedom to lovers in the forest, which is traditionally a symbol of confusion and an obstacle upon life's journey.' *Genesis*, the first reproduction in the book, is an image of considerable potency. Skelton's analysis of the iconography is convincing. 'The butterfly,' he writes, 'is a traditional image of the soul. The snake may be the serpent of psychic energy, or that which worked its will in the garden of Eden. I suspect the flower to be a sunflower, which is therefore a symbol of time. The lady and her child clearly suggest birth. As the snake is also phallic masculine and the bloom of the flower is often used as an image for female genitals, we have here a possible picture of the act of conception and its consequences.'

While Eros presides over many of the images chosen for the book, and Thanatos is given a couple, there are others with purely metaphysical implications. *Divination* (number 24), for instance, could be a segment in a Jungian dream analysis. An isolated door stands before a circle of light, while in the foreground there lies a dish containing a stone surrounded by water. Skelton's comment is, 'One method of divination is to stare into a bowl of oil, or into water that is covering a polished black stone. The door here is obviously at once leading to and obscuring the light of knowledge or illumination.'

Not all the images are to be taken with deadly seriousness. Skelton is, after all, turning to collage not only as a way of giving vent to his need for visual creativity but also as a release and a relaxation after the rigours of serious writing. Occasionally, as in *The Game* (number 45), one suspects he is deliberately 'hamming it up'. One hears the characteristic fruity chuckle.

From an art critic's point of view, the collages stand up well. When a critic labels a painting 'literary' he usually does so in a pejorative sense, meaning that its anecdotal details are given preference at the expense of the overall coherence of the composition. In this sense there is nothing literary about Skelton's work. He thinks basically as a painter. His designs are strong, sure, and admirably varied.

While living in Manchester, Robin and his wife Sylvia made a handsome contribution to the life of that city by organizing public art exhibitions. It was due to him, for instance, that Manchester enjoyed its first open-air sculpture show. Once settled in Victoria, they began to do their bit for the arts community there. While

'The Game', collage, Robin Skelton.

Sylvia contributed knowledgeable enthusiasm and quietly efficient organizing ability to the women's committee of the city's art gallery, and later to its arts council, Robin began vigorously to enlarge the art collection they had jointly begun in Britain. This time they concentrated mainly on the leading painters and sculptors of the Victoria area. In later years, as Robin began to make the acquaintance of artists living in Ireland and in the American northwest, the collection grew to contain a substantial representation of work from those two areas.

Robin's career as a public donor began in the 1960s with gifts to the Art Gallery of Greater Victoria and the organization of a fund drive from which purchases were made of the works of Victoria artists in memory of Michael Dane, a university professor. Next, in 1980, came a major gift to the University of Victoria's Maltwood Art Museum of forty-nine lithographs, etchings, and woodcuts by contemporary Irish artists. The following year the university received from him and Sylvia twenty-three prints by Jack Yeats, the artist brother of William Butler. During these years he was also serving the Art Gallery of Greater Victoria as a member of its board of directors.

It would have been surprising had he failed to use his great gifts as a writer to promote those areas of the visual arts where his tastes and feelings were most passionately engaged. In fact, he made signal contributions in two media. In the 1960s he became the weekly art critic of the Victoria Daily Times. In his lively and sometimes controversial columns he used this platform to further the interests of the leading artists of Vancouver Island and of the avant garde generally. His espousal of the cause of the best local talent took its most lasting form, however, in the shape of monographs in *The Malahat Review*. There, with the help of high-quality reproductions, he analyzed the work of such talents as Maxwell Bates, Richard Ciccimarra, Elza Mayhew, Myfanwy Pavelic, Robert de Castro, and Herbert Siebner.

For the last-named artist he has long felt a special affinity, one result of which was the production of two collaborative books, *Inscriptions* and *Musebook,* both of which contained Robin's poems with illustrations by Siebner. Both are limited edition collectors' items. In 1979 he wrote a monograph to accompany a retrospective show of Siebner's work at The Maltwood Art Museum.

Where, amid his teaching duties and his prolific activities as poet, writer of books, magazine editor, and critic Robin has found time for his abundant production as a collagist is something of a mystery. Possibly it is a mystery to him too.

Marion Rippon
A Few Words on Robin

RECOLLECTIONS? Forever vivid! But in a few words? Impossible!

Still ... University of Victoria campus. A wartime hut converted into offices. Smeared windows filtering June heat onto absolute chaos. Somewhere at the far end of a tunnel of books, papers, manuscripts, a British voice, possibly hiding a smile. Spectacles, wild streaked brown beard and hair. Fingers, heavy with unique rings, gesture. 'Push some of that stuff somewhere and find a chair.' Probably thinking, what does this middle-aged bleached blonde know about teaching writing? With a degree in nursing? Deliver me from amateurs!

I wasn't prepared to stay long enough to sit. I'd left my husband in the car outside, motor running. 'I'll just be a second,' I'd said. 'I'm not letting any crazy genius poet fire me before I have a chance to quit.'

Still, I was curious. So I squatted on the edge of something, my credentials clutched in a plastic grocery bag on my knee. Besides, I'd spent a long time dressing for the occasion: long, bright, homemade dress and clogs on bare feet. I hadn't been on a campus for thirty years, but I was determined not to be outdone by hordes of scruffy kids and a long-haired professor.

I'd been warned. The director of the Correspondence Branch for the BC Department of Education had asked me to continue as instructor for a new course in creative writing. But, he said, Professor Skelton, who was contracted to write the course, had insisted on approving the writer who would be correcting and grading the students' work. Would I at least agree to meet with the professor? I, with two Doubleday Crime Club novels published and a third already accepted?

So here we were. The beard spoke again. 'Would you like to look over the first new correspondence course lessons? I haven't had time to complete them all.'

I didn't want to like the voice, but there was warmth now, and that touch of humour. For some inexplicable reason I offered him my plastic bag of Crime Club writing, cleared a space on a nearby table, accepted a fresh-from-the-printer LESSON 1, and we both began to read.

At about LESSON 111 I looked up suddenly, and asked him, 'Have you a degree in psychology?'

It was then I heard THE LAUGH for the very first time. It is indescribable – a jolly sort of Canada goose chortle that erupts from a loving, joyous well deep inside the man. It's enveloping and addictive.

No, he told me. He just liked people. He just knew people. And I began to know that I was reading, discovering, the best guide to creative writing that had ever been designed, and that I desperately wanted to be a part of it.

I kept reading. 'Write a conversation between yourself as a child and yourself as an adult.' Brilliant! The solution to solving the hurdle of believable dialogue, and providing a revelation – invaluable to an instructor – of the personality of each student.

There were no RIGHT or WRONG 'answers' on any of the papers. They were exercises in stimulating the imagination, a guiding, a shepherding of aspiring writers into the world of fiction, of poetry – the whole limitless world of words.

He had moved to the door. Coffee? Oh yes, please. No, I'd never had the opportunity to take a creative writing course. I just loved to write, had to write – so I did, and I got lucky. Of course I had more time today, and yes, I'd like to talk.

Then suddenly the realization of time, and a car motor running. 'Would you excuse me while I run outside and tell my husband not to wait, he can come back later?'

And my dear friend Robin laughed again because he knew. He reads minds too. That was a lifetime ago, and you ask for memories of him in a few words? I join in his laughter.

Susan Musgrave
A Beard in The Bay Pavilion

I DON'T THINK I'd even seen a beard before. I'd certainly heard of them from my maiden aunt who called them 'appendages' and said they defied conjecture. She also said they never failed to excite uncommon sensations. Robin's certainly did, the second time I laid eyes on him near Admissions in Victoria's Bay Pavilion, the psychiatric wing of the Royal Jubilee Hospital, 1967. The nurses were so excited, in fact, they failed to notice when I spat out my anti-depressants.

It was springtime. I had just celebrated my sixteenth birthday. I'd dropped out of high school and dropped enough acid to need a rest for awhile. The Bay Pavilion was where people came to rest, another patient told me, not in the final sense but at least for a spring vacation.

Robin had met my psychiatrist, Dr. Gregory ('you, Dr. Gregory, walk from breakfast to madness') at a drinks party. Dr. Gregory told him about the young girl ensconced in Room o (Kafka would have loved it) who was writing poetry. As it turned out, I'd baby-sat the Skeltons' young children before (that was the *first* time I'd laid eyes on him) so we'd already had an introduction. I remembered the Skeltons' house because there was Art and there were Books (we had books at home, but these were ones *Robin* had written).

I gave my pills to a depressed hairstylist who ran off a week later, to Port Angeles with someone else's husband. Robin swept the nurses aside with his briefcase. And his beard. He could have had a file hidden in all that face, something to break me out with. He *did* break me out that day, in a different kind of way.

We drank tea in the canteen. Robin would preferred something stronger, but booze was about the only drug we didn't have access to in that place. He asked to see some of my poetry and I gave him my most recent work, which I'd managed to type out on the typewriter my father had bought in Cairo before the war. In lieu of a metaphor, I would throw in the odd hieroglyphic. My high school teacher had called me 'avant-garde'.

When Robin left he gave me a copy of *Howl* and a copy of *Ariel* (my first poems had been influenced by Tennyson and Bob Dylan) – causing critics, in the future, to label me 'the chance daughter of Allen Ginsberg and Sylvia Plath'. Chance? I'm not so sure about that. Jung says, 'Coincidence, if traced back far enough, becomes inevitable.'

Robin at Mannin Bay, West Ireland 1983.

Robin took six of my poems for publication in *The Malahat Review* and with my first cheque ($100) I bought my first typewriter. My *own* typewriter. Without hieroglyphics. (Critics, in the future, were to note a marked change.)

Robin also gave me a list of literary magazines where he suggested I send my poems, to 'harden the heart as the might lessens'. Get used to rejections. (Does anyone *get used* to rejection?) I submitted. Five of the seven magazines accepted poems.

I saw very little of Robin after that. The reports of our affairs are greatly exaggerated. I was never his protégée, student, lover, housekeeper, spiritual advisor, dental mechanic or good luck charm. Occasionally we had lunch together at the Faculty Club where he would make the appropriate noises over my poems, between mouthfuls of chewed beard and Yago Blanco, and once we went to St. Ives. With his whole family. Robin, it turned out, was the man with seven wives. Or was that only another rumour? (In Victoria, you can start a rumour for two dollars and fifty cents. But it will cost you two hundred and fifty dollars to stop it. Robin, I think, had something to do with the establishment of this service, but then again that might be only a rumour, too.)

In 1983 we were chosen to tour Ireland together, an External Affairs / Writers' Union sponsored trip. Three weeks of readings in twenty-one towns, and we're still speaking to each other, even after that. But no, there is no truth to the rumour (I heard it in Toronto) that Charlotte, my very blonde, very blue-eyed daughter, is a by-product of that tour. She doesn't have the same chin – though how can I say that for sure never having seen his?

That day in the Bay Pavilion marked a whole new direction in my life. I met a lot of people with beards after that, and I have Art on my walls, now, and Books that I have written. If it hadn't been for Robin I might still be writing in hieroglyphics, or regurgitating Tennyson in Room 0. I might have chosen a life of quiet desperation in the suburbs of Los Angeles, eating anti-depressants out of a real need, and feeding them to my 3.2 children. I might have married a banker, instead of a man who robs them, but somehow I doubt it. I might have gone to law school, lived like a wretch and died rich. If it hadn't been for Robin. Which much of it is.

Lala Heine-Koehn
The Rust-Red Grown Beds

for Robin, who made me do it.

(Cynghanedd)

Autumn leaves falling, autumn loves failing,
the green beds of old are the grown buds fled.
A rainy tree, long strands of rain trailing,
a wish, a word, a cry: Wash away red!

John Barton
Suddenly Glancing Up From My Book

I TINKERED WITH 'Suddenly Glancing Up From My Book' for about two years before actually completing it. The red coat of a friend of mine, the poem's initial inspiration, combined with a memory of another woman in red I once glimpsed by chance from a window at the University of Victoria library; she was crossing the quad on a very rainy day. I could never quite shake the response it provoked in me, yet I could never pin it down either. As a result the poem never went anywhere and I often abandoned it in frustration.

One day, however, I noticed that the voice speaking it was one I knew but could not identify. It was barely audible at first, but as I began working on the poem, changing one word for another, altering images, stresses, and line breaks, I heard it gradually enunciate each line more clearly, each syllable lingering on the tongue. The voice was low, considered, resonant; when I realized it was Robin's I worked more consciously to catch it and the poem fell into line with little protest.

I was a student of Robin's for three years. That was over four years ago, yet I am only now beginning to recognize the extent of his influence. It is not something that can be summarized in words for it feels more like an instinct. The best I can do is write words around it like the circles opening from the pebble in the last two couplets. Besides the techniques that Robin taught me constantly surfacing, I feel there is something else of him here. It is an attitude, a way of seeing, a set of magical associations first perceived in the world, then reflected and completed through language.

Suddenly Glancing Up From My Book

after Robin Skelton

All week: sun
dazzled rain.

Outside this
afternoon

window, arbutus
branches spread

like wings out
of the mist,

A leaf breaks loose.
Sunlit it falls,

settles as a rail
might each foot

crossing a pool.
A woman crosses

the lawn
in carnation red

stockings.
The remark of her

heel against
a stone

cast long ago
unlinks from it

in rings as if
the stone were

dropping brightly
through water.

Marilyn Bowering
Notes

1. ROBIN SKELTON'S BELT, 'The Walrus and the Carpenter', coiled on my typewriter rather than wrapped around a chair as it appeared next to the chapter, 'Conspiracy' in my 1979 book, *The Visitors Have All Returned*. A belt no self-respecting academic or serious poet would own up to, but the property of the salacious *Zuk*, perhaps, or the maker of those disturbing art-collages; shifting beneath his formidable persona, looking out of the corners of his eyes a little sly and amused.

MICHAEL ELCOCK

2. Here is my 1970 poem, and with it a photograph of the collage
Robin showed me as soon as he had finished reading it. The first of
many demonstrations of his finely tuned psychic antennae.

The Fisherman's Dream   71

I see her
on the ice
moving in silver
bringing stars down.

There are days
when men drown.
I see her
she walks this way.

There is no where to go
no where I would,
but I hide from this woman
who crosses the ice
like a girl
becoming a bride.

MICHAEL ELCOCK

3. Robin's *Advice To A Young Poet*: a summary of seminars 1970-72.

Learn the craft with all the abilities at your disposal.
Take pride in your mastery of forms.
Turn your hand to anything: the first law of poetry is survival.
Respect the Muse: your health and safety depend upon it.
Learn punctuation.
Feed on mythology, science, art. Keep your hands busy.
Always invent, always make.

4. For his fiftieth birthday Robin wrote 'Fifty Syllables'. I offer this, appropriated from David Malouf (further advice: steal, but acknowledge). The title counts too.

For Robin at Sixty

I am
face to face
with something that is not
myself or of my own making,
something that belongs to another order of being
and which I come out of the depths of myself to meet
as at the surface of a glass.

Peter Robinson
The Absolute Holiness of the Task:
Robin Skelton's Writings on the Art of Poetry

'I believe in technique as the test of man's sincerity.'
Ezra Pound.

BETWEEN 1971 AND 1978, Robin Skelton published three books on poetry – *The Practice of Poetry*, a valuable manual, useful both for the writing and teaching of the art; *The Poet's Calling,* an examination of poetry as a profession; and *Poetic Truth,* a philosophical inquiry into the nature of poetry. The books differ in intention, but one thread can be discerned running throughout all three: the author's attempt to define the poet's nature and his function in contemporary society. Skelton also appears to be thinking out and defining his own commitment to the 'sullen art', and while the books certainly instruct and delight the reader, they also reveal the author's own search for answers to the questions he confronts.

The books form a trilogy in that their development is not merely linear; often, a later volume will pick up on an idea introduced earlier and discuss it either in more depth or from a different perspective. The first book, for example, deals with poetic metre and includes a useful guide to verse technique, and the third demonstrates how certain words can be given emotional resonance through cunning metrical arrangement. Throughout the three, Skelton continually demonstrates how emotion, intellect and imagination are inseparably linked with technique. This position is especially refreshing these days, when most poetry seems to be the result of unfettered self-expression or differs from prose only in the variety of its margins.

Skelton not only emphasizes how essential it is for the poet to know about rhyme, metre and stanza forms – what he calls 'the technology of verse' – but he also takes an obvious delight in writing about such matters, just as he clearly takes pleasure in the formal elements of his own poetry and approaches, say, the George Faludy translations as a metrical challenge.

My concern here is with the value of the books to poets, and any discussion from this perspective must concentrate on *The Practice of Poetry* and *The Poet's Calling,* as *Poetic Truth* is chiefly slanted toward readers. The first two books emphasize the importance of technique and outline the necessary depth and strength of the poet's commitment. To writing about these two subjects, Skelton brings both his own experience and, through solicited quotations and worksheets, the experience of poets such as John Montague, Thomas Kinsella, Tony Connor, Kathleen Raine, Theodore Roethke and Robert Graves.

The Practice of Poetry, with its chatty, informal style and varied exercises, seems designed as much for the classroom as for the lone practitioner. In his preface, Skelton explains how he searched for 'a book that combines technical instruction in verse craftsmanship with instruction in the manipulation of the imagination and the development of the individual poetic vision.' Unable to find such a book, he wrote it himself.

The first chapter, 'Finding the Word Hoard', is designed to stimulate the imagination. Skelton insists that poets must give themselves 'freedom, even perhaps the irresponsibility, to let things develop'. Yet it is soon made clear that unless what develops is given form and pattern, it will not become a poem. Yes, the 'verbal excitement' must be discovered and generated unself-consciously, but 'the writing of poetry is as much a matter of arranging verbal excitements as of discovering them.' This is the essential step that, unfortunately, so many poets choose to ignore.

When it comes to the basics of verse, Skelton very sensibly notes that students are often introduced to complicated forms too soon and should instead be led slowly from the simplest effects of folk poetry to more sophisticated exercises. He introduces readers to the underlying principles of all poetic patterns – repetition and variation – instead of laboriously listing the individual forms in all their complicated incarnations. Put this way, it doesn't seem such a long journey from ballad to sestina; even less does it seem an unusual and exacting demand that poets should make the trip.

Common sense is one of the chief virtues of Skelton's approach to poetics. So often children seem to learn at school that rhythm and metre are fixed matters; no one points out that all readers would fall asleep in two minutes or less if iambic pentameter really did consist of line after line of pentametric iambs.

As Skelton notes, most of our assumptions about metre are based on those of the Latin and Greek poets from whom we took our descriptive terms. Their prosody, however, applied to quantitative verse, where the length of the syllable was of prime importance. Though almost all poets have realized it, few teachers seem to have understood how important it is that ours is a language of stress and that, consequently, quantitative metre rarely works well in English. As Derek Attridge says in his attempt to remodel English prosody, *The Rhythms of English Poetry*, 'Our shelves are heavy with handbooks for the schoolroom parading lists of Greek terms and recherché metres culled from Swinburne and Bridges.' Skelton, too, debunks the old teaching at the outset and replaces it with the ear's common sense: 'A line of verse must be capable of being spoken aloud with ease and in such a manner that the speaker remains a credible human being.'

Skelton is also insistent on the value of the various forms of poetry and their relation to personal vision: 'It is, perhaps, only when one has mastered rhyme, rhythm, diction and some abstract forms that one can begin to discover one's own individual vision, for that vision, if one is a poet, is inseparable from the poetry itself.'

It is around chapter seven, 'Staying in Business', that other concerns, perhaps dormant earlier, begin to surface, and questions leading directly to the next two books are raised. However much formal grounding they have, poets must somehow still keep in touch with their imaginations if they are to continue writing, and Skelton has suggested a number of exercises and procedures, such as the journal, to aid in this process. But, perhaps giving voice to personal concerns, he now goes even further and states that 'it is important ... to recognize that poetry involves a life-discipline, and not merely a discipline of the mind.'

Though Skelton writes that 'poets are no different from other people, except in their training themselves to notice all their own sensations,' it is clear that the degree of their commitment to poetry does, somehow, separate them from others, and Skelton does not overlook the madness, despair, insanity and suicide that often plague poets in their isolation.

Skelton raises an important distinction here: that between the 'poet' and the 'maker of poems'. 'If one is not possessed by a sense of the overriding importance of making poems; if one is not compelled to make them, and if one does not discipline one's life in terms of poetry, then one is not, perhaps a poet, though one may make poems and some of them may be good.' It is here that Skelton begins to examine the nature of the poet's commitment. 'There is nothing wrong with being a maker of poems rather than a poet,' he continues. 'There is, indeed, much to be said for it, and many of our finest works have been created by such people.' What, then, is the difference between the poet and the maker of fine poems? How can we decide who belongs to which category? We can't, of course, and that is why the problem is so intriguing. Only the writer himself knows, and, as the poet's life is rarely one of constant certainty and self-confidence, even he or she might not always be sure.

One can, perhaps, take the compulsion to write poetry as a

guide. If poets are 'possessed by the overriding importance of making poems,' then they will often, if not always, be engaged in that essential activity. Can we, therefore, take production figures as yardstick?

If we do, we might say, for example, that Philip Larkin was not, according to Skelton's definition, a poet, but a maker of poems. Had he been a poet, he would not have settled for so little. He wrote hardly any poems at all in the last ten years, complaining that poetry had given him up, and not vice versa. Should Larkin perhaps have carried out poetic exercises to loosen his imagination? Should he have kept a journal? Wouldn't he have done *anything*, surely, just to keep the poems coming?

Obviously it is not only difficult but also foolish to attempt such judgements. Nonetheless, the distinction between poet and maker of poems remains vague and puzzling until one turns to *The Poet's Calling*, where Skelton expounds upon the idea.

The poet must be committed to his art above all else. Human relationships often go by the wayside: 'There are even instances of poets bringing their mistresses home to meet their wives, convinced by the intensity of their belief that what excites them to poetry cannot be anything but admirable.' Health, wealth (certainly!) and perhaps even sanity may also be sacrificed to the Muse – but whatever it costs, the poet will make poems. Larkin didn't. Was he, therefore, not a poet but a maker of poems?

On the other hand, Geoffrey Hill, for example, has not produced a great quantity of poetry, but his work is of a staggering intensity; he is known to write slowly and with great difficulty. Hill once said about the subject, 'I have known inspiration, but only at the end of a work as a result of exhaustion and near-despair. I think exhaustion is a great begetter of inspiration: sheer tiredness breaks down certain barriers of the conscious mind. There is that marvellous remark of Yeats' about a poem coming together with a click like a closing box which is, I think, an almost perfect description of that moment of ecstatic completion, when the last true word you've been seeking with weariness and with near despair for so long, finally and miraculously moves into place.' These words have the same tenor as many of the quotations Skelton draws on in *The Poet's Calling*, and few would deny that Hill is a poet rather than a maker of poems.

Ultimately, though, does it really matter whether the writer is a poet or a maker of poems? Perhaps from the reader's or critic's perspective it doesn't, but from the poet's viewpoint it is of vital importance, and that is why Skelton devotes so much time and argument to the nature and extent of the poet's commitment. He quotes Kathleen Raine on the subject: ' "Thou shalt have no other gods before me!" It doesn't matter what. You can put anything before your poetry and that will be quite sufficient to destroy it. It may be the most high-sounding things like family obligations – one must put one's children before one's work – well, in that case perhaps one shouldn't have married and had children.'

If, at the start of *The Poet's Calling*, Skelton appears to be putting forward a romantic view of the poet as a man possessed, his eyes in a 'fine frenzy rolling', he does not neglect the value of technique for long: 'Poetry is an "art" and a "mystery", but is also a craft.... Concern for the craft of verse goes hand in hand with concern for the full exploration and presentation of poetic vision.'

One goal of *The Poet's Calling* is to give poets and poetry the status Skelton believes they deserve, and this is another reason why the distinction between poet and maker of poems is important. The book works as a tonic for any poet who feels doubt about the worth of his or her vocation, which Skelton describes as 'a dignified and learned profession, a "high mystery", rather than a trivial game of emotional assertion and vulgar pretensions.'

Near the end of *The Practice of Poetry*, Skelton writes that 'the practice of poetry itself constitutes a faith and a belief,' and it is through looking at poetry in terms of religion, an idea he examines in more depth in *The Poet's Calling*, that he comes closest to distinguishing the poet from the maker of poems.

The poet's is a mystical and religious art with close links to the world of magic, myth and dreams. Poetry, for one so committed, is a religion requiring total devotion. Again, Skelton quotes Kathleen Raine: 'You must be ruthless to something and if you are permissive to human relationships you are being ruthless to your poetry, and forbidding it to flower and be born, and it's a matter of what you regard as the more important. And of course for a true poet it seems to me that you must put nothing before your vocation.'

If the commitment is total, if it comes before and above all else, then one is a poet, and poetry is, indeed, one's religion. If not, one is a maker of poems. Anne Stevenson, according to a review by Peter Hainsworth in the TLS, has recently allied herself to David Jones in embracing 'a work-aesthetic in which the artist commits himself (herself) to craft almost at the expense of self ... in structures which put the harmony of parts before self-expression.' This is the kind of commitment Skelton is getting at.

In order to distinguish true and deep commitment from the mere childish relinquishing of responsibilities for a dream-world which, in Auden's words, 'makes nothing happen', Skelton builds a strong case for the importance of poetry to humanity. The problem is one of authority. Skelton asks where, these days, does a poet get his authority from; how can he convince others that he is worth reading; and what is his role in the contemporary world? As with all the other questions, there is no easy answer. Pound, Kazantzakis, W.C. Williams and Yeats are all presented as poets who confronted the problem of poetic authority and solved it in one way or another, and Skelton finally hazards an attempt at defining the poet's 'twofold' role: 'He must bring all things into unity, the past into unity with the present, the Classical with the Christian, the nationalist with the cosmic, the local with the general; and he must remake what has fallen, thus becoming at once the worker in many traditions, and the unifier of all.'

Not content to stop at even such a tall order as this, Skelton delves deeper in an attempt to grasp the 'mystery of poetry'. Though he ultimately confesses failure, he hints at a possible solution: 'The central mystery is indefinable. It can only be hinted at. It has to do with ... Muse visions ... with the poet's awareness of extra-sensory perceptions, with his profound sense of alienation (and hence, frequently, guilt), and with a burning and irrational conviction that (to use the words of Yeats), "Words alone are certain good." '

While taking on such difficult matters as the poet's function and the mystery at the heart of poetry, Skelton also manages to keep in touch with the more practical matters, like the pros and cons of academic jobs for poets, and he also injects some humour into a discussion of poets such as Louis MacNeice, Shelley, Yeats and Gerard de Nerval, who all invented eccentric social characters either as attention-getting devices or as cloaks for hypersensitivity. These poets all created strange personae through their odd clothes, weird habits, or unusual pets. De Nerval, for example, 'promenaded Paris with a lobster on a string,' while Shelley 'took to carrying pistols and indulging in target practice.'

Finally, though, the import of the book is serious and moving, and Skelton is painfully aware that merely dressing eccentrically does not make a man a poet: 'The poet is one who devotes his whole life to this activity, and does so in the teeth of social opposition or, at best, indifference, and despite much emotional and mental disturbance. He must be very strong if he is to continue for a whole lifetime, and he must tell himself over and over again, for few others will tell him, that the job is worth doing. He must, in humility, revering the vocation itself and not the follower of the vocation, follow Theodore Roethke's advice to himself: Remind yourself once more of the absolute holiness of your task.' There is a degree of intensity in the rhythms and cadences of this passage unusual in a book of this nature. Clearly, the words have not only been thought but also lived and felt. Indeed, it seems that Skelton is, throughout the entire three books, defining his own position – reminding himself of Roethke's advice – and nowhere is this more evident than in *The Poet's Calling*.

It is difficult to convince oneself that a vocation for poetry is worthwhile when the pleasures are, more often than not, private and hard-earned, while the humiliations are usually public and all too easily come by, and Skelton's description of his twelve years as a university professor at Manchester provides a daunting example of the kinds of contumely the poet must face: 'Never once in that twelve years did the University ask me to give a reading of my work, and one of my colleagues made it a habit of leaving the Staff Lounge whenever some incautious visitor committed the social gaffe of referring to my poetry. Although I was at that time the only member of the faculty who had published a book of poems of any kind ... I was never invited to meet any of those visiting poets whose visits I had not myself arranged.' It is probably an understatement when he concludes, 'I found that this treatment did my work no good at all. I grew progressively depressed.'

If I have dwelt on *The Poet's Calling* at great length, it is because that book seems, to me, to be the core of the trilogy. In it, Skelton faces all the doubts and problems he knows other poets face and sails a dangerous course between the Scylla of inflated self-importance and the Charybdis of false modesty, generally managing to avoid both. He also reiterates his belief in the importance of technique and craft, expressed in such detail in the first book.

In *The Practice of Poetry*, Skelton observes that the poet, when unable to write, may feel 'wracked with guilt over his selfishness and feel that his whole life has been wasted in the pursuit of a will o' the wisp. At such times it is hard for anyone to help him.' These books do help, though, and that is surely achievement enough.

Christopher Wiseman
Robin Skelton

I FIRST HEARD OF Robin Skelton in the 1950s when my father, a professor at Manchester University, would come home with stories of a young lecturer whose behaviour and attitudes were causing some consternation among the more staid of the faculty. This man, a poet, ruffling complacent feathers, caught my imagination (and my father's), and the name of Robin Skelton was often heard in our house. I can't remember when I first read any of his poetry – not long after hearing these stories, I suppose – but I recall being surprised at how non-rebellious, graceful and tender the poems were, and wondering if the offended old-guard at the university had ever bothered to read them.

When I arrived in Calgary in the late 1960s, I knew of Robin's being in Victoria, of the creative writing programme he had started there, but I didn't in fact meet him until the mid 1970s. I was talking to Kathleen Raine, the British poet, and she was insistent that I look him up, that we had much in common in addition to the similar trajectories which had taken us both from the coast of Yorkshire, to Manchester, to the United States, to western Canada. I met him, finally, in Calgary, and liked him immediately, feeling very comfortable with him, and being impressed by his knowledge, his friendliness, his professionalism. There was not much sign of the wild young rebel who, in my teens, had been a larger-than-life figure, tearing through Victorian halls of learning leaving trails of outrage and scandal, but he was certainly, still, a highly distinctive figure. Since that meeting, I have seen him many times and consider him a friend and someone who has been extraordinarily kind and helpful. A casual remark by me at his dinner table about my frustrations with Canada's leading academic press, which had kept my book on Edwin Muir for 18 months without a word, led to his offering to look at it for a new series of critical books he was planning for Sono Nis Press. A month later it was accepted. He accepted my poetry for *The Malahat Review*, and a collection of my poetry for Sono Nis. He invited me to read at the University of Victoria as part of the book launching. He supported me in my fight to establish creative writing at the University of Calgary, and has written strong references for me. But these are externals. I can't chart a friendship this way. I must give a few impressions and memories at random.

His laugh – surely the most unique and infectious in Canada!

Laughter and wine and food around his table, Sylvia smiling at us as if we were 14. Robin sitting patiently, flanked by my children, turning their eyes to saucers by his massive stamp-collection, generously giving them often valuable duplicates. His first showing me his study – a real room for writing in that lovely old house, with the incredible Robert Graves collection, the old army uniform, the chart where he records the progress of his various writing projects. Signing one of my book contracts at a party in his house, bedlam all around. The parties, with their mixture of people, the goodwill and geniality, Robin's delight in having his friends around him. His confinement to a wheelchair with extremely painful sciatica, which didn't stop his welcoming us as if nothing were wrong, though he would cry out with the pain from time to time. His commonsense and his perceptive, intelligent remarks at League of Canadian Poets meetings before he resigned in frustration. The quality of his poetry readings, both as performance and as moving literary experience. His father's pride the night of his daughter's first art show. His wide-ranging mind – from gritty Yorkshire realism all the way to the numinous, the supernatural. The generosity of his encouragement to his students and all young writers. Reading his *Collected Shorter Poems* and knowing in my gut, sadly and resentfully, that this book would have walked away with the Governor General's Award had Robin been born in Canada or been from a more fashionable ethnic background. Sitting watching 'Yanks' with him on TV, each of us trying to pick out buildings and landscapes we'd known long years ago. His enormous literacy in art, in music, as well as in literature. Spending an afternoon with him cataloguing his hundreds of old 78 records, listening to music I hadn't heard for 30 years or more. His writing, consistently underrated. The 70-odd books. His energy. And much much more. But mainly his warmth. That laugh!

David Watmough
The Truth of the Matter

WITH ROBIN SKELTON there is never any catching up to do. One month, six months, even a year – the hiatus never plays havoc with continued threads of talk and the easeful glow of friendship.

The venue for all this, at least for me, is likely to be a bar, the invariable constituents John Jamesons or Bushmills: an asseveration of the superiority of Irish to Scotch and then, probably, a mutual reassurance of ongoing affection for churchyards, graveyards, cemeteries and their common inhabitants. We have a ghoulish link.

I met this Brobdingnagian version of 'Doc' (from the Disney version of the Wagnerian dwarfs) as a result of shared membership in the earlier days of the life of the Writers' Union of Canada. But I learned of his reputation as a poet, as a teacher, friend and, above all, as an enthusiast for artistic talent – painting and poetry in particular – from a young poet of mutual acquaintance named Theresa Kishkan. She it was who persuaded me to read his poetry and it was thus I discovered the unique and exciting west coast Englishry of Robin's verse.

He raved a book of mine in review and accepted a story for *The Malahat* which he edited in its golden days. The a priori conditions of friendship between two writers fell swiftly into position when I informed him that his poetry of place, the Pacific, even the Vancouver Island place, fed me richly in its verbal felicity. We have never quarrelled.

But Robin at sixty is surely a myth. I have always considered him ninety and a father-figure – even though there is but a matter of months separating our birthdates!

Robin is a patriarchal man – beyond the beard, the Dickensian hair and the general appearance of a Havelock Ellis who has fallen on dishevelled days. He is a kindly patriarch, though. The eyes twinkle and he hears loquacious writers out. This is no stern Moses, hirsute halo notwithstanding, for our patriarch has Peter Pan lurking about his whiskers.

My friend is also a cautious creature. Robin never enters bars until he has inspected them from the doorway. I noticed once that he would not cross a room in the Faculty Club at UBC until he had tested the carpet. There is also an incredible capacity for friendly communication co-habiting with a distinct shyness in this odd amalgam. I entered a cool and stygian bar at The Royal York

Hotel in Toronto with him one day last year. The busy and distracted waitress looked up from preparing peanuts on a table and said:

'Why, Dr. Skelton, how nice to see you again. A Bushmills, I suppose, with the usual soda?'

'An old acquaintance?' I asked. 'I guess this is one of your regular watering places.'

'No,' he said, as he inspected his seat before sitting down. 'I just met her this afternoon when I first came into this bar. A nice lass, eh? She has a good memory for life's significant things.'

But Robin is memorable – even after fifteen minutes at a bar table. That is the truth of the matter.

Robert Bringhurst
Of Gladness as a Moral Force in Time

ROBIN SKELTON ARRIVED in western Canada as a teacher soon after I, as a young student, had left it. He was an indwelling part of the literary and intellectual landscape a decade later when I returned. Others who have known him longer may speak more knowledgeably than I of his career as a poet, teacher and editor. But it is worth our while to reflect as well on his contributions as a publisher. This is my topic, though I may stray from it now and again into the wider topic of poetry – for poetry is the place where the whole man dances, in time with himself and beyond the reach of time.

We are tainted with history, all of us, and for the evils of history poetry is no cure – though it may serve at least as a contrary force, a means of restoring within and about us the balance between timelessness and time. Poetry is the place in which all men and women are contemporaries, notwithstanding the differences – stupefying and painful differences sometimes – which time and place have marked upon them. It is on that account that poetry might be worth publishing. And though it is not the only thing he has ever written or edited, poetry is indeed the only thing Robin Skelton *acting as publisher* has yet published.

Most of what I have to say concerns Robin's publishing activities in western Canada; much of what I have to say, in fact, concerns a single book. But when a fuller discussion of Robin's work as a publisher is someday written, it will have to begin with his student days, in the late 1940s, at Leeds. There his Lotus Press issued a series called the Acadine Poets and an anthology called *Leeds University Poetry 1949*. It was small-press publishing of the traditional kind: Skelton was editor, designer and publisher. He was sales manager as well, hawking his wares about the town and campus, turning them shilling by shilling into beer.

The Lotus Press folded about 1951, but over the next dozen years, as Robin occupied himself with writing, teaching and editing, he was also studying the private-press tradition. (The Irish presses, Cuala and Dolmen, seem, not surprisingly, to have been of special interest to him.) He took up publishing once again only in 1963, the year he arrived in western Canada. At unpredictable intervals since then he has issued both books and broadsides, at first in his own name, and more recently under the imprint of the Pharos Press. Over the same span, he has provoked, promoted and collaborated upon countless other publishing ventures – and for sixteen of those years served the communities of readers, of writers, and of publishers alike as editor of the best quarterly magazine in Canada, *The Malahat Review.*

I turn now to the books for which Robin has served as publisher since his arrival in North America. There are only seven of these altogether, produced over a span of twenty years. There are five authors – Skelton himself, Robert Graves, Susan Musgrave, Seán Virgo, George Faludy – and in two of the books there is also the work of one artist, Herbert Siebner. All of these books were limited editions, designed and printed in the shop of one printer, Charles Morriss of Victoria. The most recent of the lot, George Faludy's *Twelve Sonnets,* in Skelton's fine and limpid translations, went to press in the year Morriss died.

Through the 1960s, Robin published (not as writer, but as publisher) only some slim volumes of his own work, bearing no imprint except his own name. The titles are *A Valedictory Poem* (1963), *Inscriptions* (1967) and *The Hold of Our Hands: Eight Letters to Sylvia* (1968). The second of these is of special interest as his first collaboration with Herbert Siebner, whose coloured drawings are reproduced, by four-colour lithography, alongside the text.

In the early 1970s, he founded the Pharos Press, which has served as his private publishing house ever since. The first book issued under this imprint, and my favourite of the lot, is *Musebook* (1972). It too was a collaboration with Siebner; in fact it reprints four poems from the earlier *Inscriptions.* The subsequent Pharos books are Graves's *The Marmosite's Miscellany* (1975), Musgrave and Virgo's *Kiskatinaw Songs* (1977) and the Faludy *Twelve Sonnets* (1983).

In Canada since the Second World War it has been the rule and not the exception for poets of talent to function as literary publishers, and for literary presses to owe their inception to poets. We have, or have had, Louis Dudek's several presses (Contact Press, the McGill Poets, Delta Canada, D.C. Books); Gaston Miron's Editions de l'Hexagone; the House of Anansi, co-founded by Dennis Lee; Sono Nis Press, founded by J. Michael Yates; Bill Bissett's Blewointmentpress; Patrick Lane's Very Stone House; Seymour Mayne's Ingluvin Books; Gary Geddes's Quadrant Books; the Tishbooks series, published once upon a time by George Bowering and his friends; Crispin Elsted's Barbarian Press. There are dozens of such examples – symptomatic of a society in which commerce and culture, instead of keeping a civil distance from one another, have grown hysterically close together (as in the case of best-seller books and popular music) or (as in the case of poetry) schizophrenically far apart.

The work of these postwar poet-publishers, of whom Robin is one of the eldest, is of several kinds and many qualities, and a rough taxonomy may be worthwhile. Restricting ourselves to western Canada for a moment, we can see at least three distinct traditions of literary publishing.

There is the guerrilla gestetner school – the quick, usually dirty and often artless sort of neoexpressionist publishing which seems to have reached the peak of its virtue in the 1960s and 1970s. *Tish* magazine is an example; so are the books which issued from Blewointmentpress and Talonbooks in their earlies days, and from Patrick Lane's Very Stone House.

Secondly, there is patronage publishing, which has had two lives. In its first life, in the 1930s, the patronage was private and focussed primarily through two Vancouver printing firms, Clarke & Stuart and Roy Wrigley.* Another enlightened printer, Charles Morriss, renewed this tradition in the 1960s, but no one at that date chose to follow his example. In its second life, patronage publishing has relied almost entirely on public money, disbursed through the Canada Council. On the west coast, the practitioners of this sort of publishing include Talonbooks, Porcépic, Oolichan and Sono Nis. (Robin, of course, was editorial director of the last for several years after Richard Morriss acquired it, in 1976, from its founder, J. Michael Yates.)

Finally, there is a modest private-press tradition, whose incarnations past and present include the Klanak Press, Takao Tanabe's Periwinkle Press, Barbarian Press, and Pharos itself.

There are other traditions of literary publishing which haven't yet flourished in western Canada. There is, in particular, the Canadian Hybrid Tradition, an artful and distinctive cross-breeding of public subsidy, craftsmanly devotion, literary insouciance and advanced photographic technology. The father of this tradition is Stan Bevington, and its birthplace, therefore, is Rochdale College in downtown Toronto, where Bevington first

---

*Wrigley was western Canada's only important literary publisher before the War, and his list would merit rereading. Clarke & Stuart came to its lesser but more notorious place in literary history through a later episode. In the 1940s, forgetting its own earlier interest in literary publishing, the firm pulped nearly all the copies of Al Purdy's first book of poems because the author had failed to pay for them.

took up printing. Its principal avatars, all even now in Ontario, are The Coach House Press and the house and clients of the Porcupine's Quill. Robin knows this tradition, of course, and admires it deeply. He accordingly once asked Tim Inkster at the Quill to design and print a book which he, Skelton, would publish. But this plan evaporated in the face of Inkster's own proprietary enthusiasm for publishing, and the book (its title was *Limits*) was finally issued under the imprint of the Porcupine's Quill. Pleased and frustrated at the same time, Robin did then what only Robin would have the energy and ingenuity to do: he established the Malahat Design Awards, of which Tim Inkster, not surprisingly, has since received the major share.

Another tradition which might take root in western Canada but hasn't is that of the livre d'artiste. A few books which I'd put in this category have actually been produced in British Columbia, but hardly enough that one could call it a live tradition. The finest example to date is a Pharos Press book I've already mentioned: the *Musebook* of 1972. It contains 39 poems by Robin Skelton and 28 drawings by Herbert Siebner, and it merits closer examination.

The poems are printed in black using Intertype Baskerville, with Emil Rudolf Weiss's Series II capitals, set by hand, for the titles. The drawings are printed, also in black, by photolithography from the pencil and ink originals, then individually hand-coloured by Siebner with ochre and blue water-base paints. The sweep of the wet brush arcing across the paper has left its trace not only in colour; the sheets, which are text-weight Strathmore, have dried into low relief. So the hand-coloured drawings possess the same kind of subtle sculptural character as the facing pages of letterpress.

Combining the fictive and anhydrous immortality of print with the fugitive immediacy of watercolour, the book is well in line with Siebner's expressed desire to create a work of art that looks 'either as if it had been made just that moment or as if it had always existed, and perhaps both.'

Musebook balances another pair of contradictory impulses as well. Photolithography, like other industrial processes, squares things off and irons them out. Here, the live watercolour resuscitates Siebner's vigorous, totemic drawings, yet the book still retains enough printerly character that it seems to belong in its binding, and it possesses a virtue very rare in hand-coloured books: it seems to ask not just to be looked at but to be read. It is 64 pages, casebound, 23 x 30.5 cm, and there were 125 numbered, signed, hand-coloured copies. Robin advertised them

– and for six months sold them – for all of $ 18.00 apiece.*

The poems in *Musebook* are not by any means Robin's best, but they speak nonetheless for one of the central themes in his work. Extensive and various though it is, Robin's poetry is very often that of a man in mind of a woman. Even his books on the craft and theory of poetry steer by this light; they are all about ecstasy and technique. He is a poet of sexual love, and like Jalal ud-Din Rumi and Juan de la Cruz and a poet we now confuse with King Solomon, he knows of the manifold meaning of sexual love. This is the import even of his poem (not from the *Musebook*) called 'Thirteen Ways of Looking at a Black Mackintosh'. Here we read:

> A man with a woman
> Is glad.
> A man with a woman in a black mackintosh
> Is glad.

The lines on which these are modelled, you'll remember, say:

> A man and a woman
> Are one.
> A man and a woman and a blackbird
> Are one.

But oneness is not enough for Robin. In his world, oneness is mere philosophy. Gladness – which has less to do with completion than with potential and memory – is all.

Musebook celebrates the muse made woman, the woman made flesh, the flesh made passionate, and the passion yielding gladness rather than violence. Always an aptitude for gladness is visible, even in poems of disappointment. (There are no poems of despair.) Yet it is not gladness without frustration, and they are not all poems of ecstasy. One of the best of these poems, I think, is a little lyric called 'The Promise':

> When she insists
> she'll be your friend
> 'for ever', hopes
> you feel the same,

*There was also a photo-offset, paperbound edition in which the drawings were reproduced in black and white. This is the version which now turns up in the second-hand bookstores.

and, with a parting
kiss on cheek,
absolves herself
of any blame,

then realize
that you have touched
the woman in
her woman's skin,
and now, part father
and part child,
belong to all
her murdered kin.

'The poet insists upon our participation in language,' he says
somewhere; while 'the grammarian, technologist, and logician
demand that we subject ourselves to it.' In the decade I've known
Robin, that distinction has been crucial to him. It is not the lonely
joy of the autocrat (nor of the author!), but the shared joy and
mystery of love and of language that he has preached and
practised all the while. *Musebook* is a beguiling and sensuous
volume, yet it is the antithesis of pornography, for its theme is
transcendent participation, not subjugation. And it speaks of the
gladness which moves outward from, more than the lust which
pulls inward toward, union. Not oneness – which sooner or later
is always authoritarian – but gladness, which is to come together
close enough to share.

I think it was the same predisposition which led Robin into his
fondness for Nikolai Berdyaev's 'ethics of creativity' as opposed to
the Pauline ethics of law. We must *create* the good, said Berdyaev,
and we must transform the evil into good, not waste our time on
the mere destruction of evil. It is a sane creed for an artist –
especially an artist like Skelton or Siebner, both of them
immigrants to Canada, both refugees, though both were fleeing
not Europe itself but the repetitive closed mythology of the
European War. There is a poem called 'The Reliquary', dedicated
to Siebner, and composed soon after Robin arrived in this country.
'Our fathers were both Artillerymen,' it begins,

both at Ypres.
Defeated, you were a prisoner,
and I the same
in my victorious desert.

>   ....
>   I show you the box from home.
>
>   These are mutual relics.
>
>   ....
>   My father kept everything....
>
>   ....
>   Ruin is our familiar.
>   To him it was strange.

This coast, where that poem was written, has only recently been joined in the conspiracy of anthropocentric time and history. Our literature still quarrels with itself on the central question of whether it too will join in that history, or will live a furtive, guerrilla existence in the timeless hills. We so misread the world, Berdyaev says, that we think everything is outside of everything else. We think truth is mere congruence, when truth is actually transformation, a breaking through.

Such a transformation – of time into timelessness, of goddess into woman, of men and women into joy – is the theme of the *Musebook*, and that is part of the legacy Robin Skelton has already left us. *Musebook* is the finest book of its kind yet produced in English Canada. And it really is, in the material, not the metaphorical sense, a book. It is a tactile and visual object, a work of painterly, printerly art, not just of words. It is something, therefore, which using mere words I cannot really quote from.

I will close this minor meditation, then, with a few lines from another piece, the well-known 'Night Poem: Vancouver Island'. I lament in this poem certain departures from my own sense of natural history, as I lament them in the work of another brilliant acoustician, Louis Zukofsky. (Herons, in my experience, lope through the air, they don't soar; neither black bears nor grizzlies have square teeth; and – this is Zukofsky, of course, and not Robin – elders, not alders, bear berries.) But I admire the poem nonetheless for its effort to bring the speaker to roost in the land. I admire also the form which that speaker takes. He is, or *it* is – as Robin says of one of the figures in a Siebner painting – 'sometimes almost like a diagram ... the emblem of a man and not the image of him.' In this, the figure in the poem speaks to those in the *Musebook*, where again there are not only images but emblems.

I heard Robin read the piece once, at one of those painful lunch-hour sessions arranged by a university teacher, baffled, like so many of his colleagues, by the question of where to put poetry

in the world, or even where to put it on campus. Robin read, as
best he could, against the mid-day noise and impatience within
and without the uncomfortable room. Too late in the hour, a
student asked to hear this longish poem. Robin began, but the
rustle of feet and clanging of doors in the hallway told us the bell
was about to ring, the audience about to burst like a pod of Scotch
broom. 'I'll skip,' said Robin, and he flew through the text like a
sidearmed stone. I'll skip too.

Turn in the bed, my Love.
We were a distant tribe
that died. These waters move
the history from our bones.
....
Something created here
the lives time has to eat.
Something invented time,
a wrinkle upon the sea.
....
Your mouth upon my mouth
solves nothing but is good.
Light rises from the sea
and time spreads with the light.
Put your body to mine;
we are the world we caused.

Detail from 'Robin Skelton', collage by Myfanwy Pavelic.

Ralph Gustafson
A Man Who Is a Poet

A GRAND MAN and a formidable, who has done more for the propagation of good writing in Canada than is measurable by yardstick. Assess him in terms of the spirit, of generosity and inspiration, and he is exalted – well below the angels, thankfully, well above the earthbound. He is both a man and that formidable object, a man who is a poet.

I name him as invaluable to the well-being of my own work; unshakable as an arbiter who has kept Canada aware of itself and free of solipsism; courageous editor and sensible educator; ironist and comedian.

It does me good to enumerate him. But I do away with all the years I could stand him in, dump him in the present as irreplaceable poet and friend. Long may he thrive.

Susan Walker
The Termination of Meaningless Debate

I FIRST MET Robin Skelton not at the University of Victoria, where I was enrolled in the English honours programme, but several years after my graduation, at a restaurant in Toronto where I interviewed him for *Quill & Quire*, the magazine of the Canadian book trade. Robin should have been a well-known phenomenon in Toronto publishing and literary circles, but he wasn't – despite the fact that he was probably the most published author in Canada. Even then, in 1973, he had 55 works listed on his curriculum vitae. Those members of the eastern literary establishment who *did* know who Robin Skelton was considered him a non-Canadian. In those heady days of cultural nationalism, a naturalized Canadian didn't count.

I knew who Robin Skelton was, of course: he was the central, if not the looming, figure in Victoria's literary and scholarly community. I also knew that he was known among writers and scholars in the United States and Great Britain for his poetry, his editorship of *The Malahat Review* and his Irish studies. (Once, as an undergraduate doing an exchange year at York University, I nervously approached the imposing-looking James Dickey at a faculty reception held for him. He immediately put me at my ease by complimenting me on coming from the university where his good friend Robin Skelton taught.)

But no matter what Skelton's international stature was, it didn't wash in Toronto. Robin didn't, as far as I knew, let that bother him. He soon became an important figure in the Toronto literary world too. Not satisfied with being one of Canada's most prolific authors, Skelton became its busiest. To add to his teaching and editing jobs, he joined Dick Morriss in a revival of Sono Nis Press, a small, prestigious publishing house founded by Vancouver poet J. Michael Yates. Morriss, the printer to whom Sono Nis owed the majority of its substantial debts, made Robin its editor and the two of them proceeded to publish, during the seven years of their association (1976 to 1983), a list of more than 50 titles.

Even for those who now knew Robin Skelton, his choice titles wasn't always predictable. In addition to poetry, fiction, art books and literary criticism by authors such as Susan Musgrave, Seán Virgo, Charles Lillard and Skelton himself, the Sono Nis list displayed Robin's taste for populist, sometimes downright eccentric, books, with a ready west-coast market. Among these titles were a novel by the thriller-writer Marion Rippon, a book on BC's 'Princess' ferry line, Skelton's own book on the Cariboo district, Dude Lavington's books on being a cowboy, Maurice Good's *Every Inch a Lear,* and Hazel Elves's memoir about her life as a carny.

By the late 1970s, Robin had become a familiar visitor to Toronto. For one thing, he was a regular participant at all three of the national associations that had become the pillars of the publishing and writing world: the Association of Canadian Publishers, the Canadian Periodical Publishers' Association and the Writers' Union of Canada. Those three organizations have undoubtedly benefited from Robin's membership, especially from his verbal skills in endless annual general meetings: Robin's eloquence has a gentle way of terminating meaningless debate.

Robin's name has cropped up frequently in the pages of *Quill & Quire,* not only as a book publisher and editor of the often financially-beleaguered *Malahat Review,* but also as a valued poetry reviewer. Robin's skills – honed in the review pages of *The Malahat* – at ploughing through piles of small-press poetry books and making discerning comments about each of them is not to be outdone.

But connoisseurs of the letter to the editor will perhaps appreciate most those contributions Robin has made to *Quill & Quire's* letters page. On the occasion of McClelland and Stewart's drastic reduction of its inventory, including all of Skelton's titles published with that firm, Robin wrote to complain not only about the fate of his own books, but on behalf of many other authors whose backlist titles wold no longer be for sale. His message to Jack McClelland was characteristically succinct:

> Jack be nimble
> Jack be quick
> Jack jump over the candlestick.

And the best letter *Quill & Quire* ever received about the difficulty of reading stories larded with association acronyms was submitted by Robin. In it, he named himself as the president of the newly-formed Acronym Suppression Society – ASS for short.

It is probably premature to say that Robin Skelton has retired from magazine and book publishing. In the last few years, however, he has resumed a relatively simple life – as merely an extraordinarily prolific and talented poet and author.

Leon Rooke
The Pick-Ax

SOME WOMEN IN MY CHOIR
HAVE TAKEN THE PICK-AX
TO WESTMINSTER ABBEY
AND BROUGHT IT TUMBLING DOWN

You may ask why they did not first come
to me before they jangled out and did it.
We could have quietly disputed the pros
and cons. What I would have told them
is that the pick-ax, one or sixteen, is
not the best way to go about it. There
are more fitting and advantageous ways
to expend one's energy. One's blood rises:
a Corner, indeed! It is why I am here at
Methusala's Tomb with my bulldozer. Ten
tons, but it moves dreamy as a baby.

William David Thomas
Professor Skelton's Travelling Medicine Show and Original Patented Snake Oil Extravaganza

THERE ARE MORE SIDES to Skelton than there are edges on a new penny, but how many of his admirers have witnessed 'The Great One' in action during one of Professor Skelton's Travelling Medicine Show and Original Patented Snake Oil Extravaganzas? Few indeed, I would hazard. This then, is an account of three such tours I undertook in his company through various countries at various times. The reader should be warned that some of the details and the chronological order of things have been obscured by the haze of time, imbibed tinctures and necessary discretion, but nonetheless the general effect is accurate. Looking back, those events and adventures take on the quality of a Georges Seurat painting: dots and commas of colour make up the general effect.

In looking at those years it is important to understand that Skelton's strong streak of Yorkshire puritanism makes it essential that he have a sound reason for doing something which might appear to others as frivolous at first sight. Spending money is a good example. Having found his own sweet rationale, he then goes about the task of getting his touring apparatus ready with glee and abandon.

So it was on our first escapade. I provided the rationale, for in the spring of 1974 I was awarded a grant to visit Robert Graves in Mallorca. As Robin was off to Europe on behalf of *The Malahat Review,* he deemed it a good idea to come to Spain to make the necessary introductions to the Family Graves. As it turned out, there were the usual complications about being in the right spot at the right time, so we arranged to meet in Mallorca in mid-summer.

By the time of our proposed rendezvous I was in Valencia and, after reading one of those books on how to see the entire known universe on $2.50 a day, I had concluded that the overnight ferry from Valencia to Palma would do the trick. In one of those moves that can only be classified as 'it seemed like a good idea at the time,' I took the cheapest ticket that could get me the boat ride and the chance to sit on a deck chair outside if I could find one vacant. My visions of sitting out in the balmy air, sipping wine and being entertained by young itinerants strumming guitars, were shattered by a freak storm that brought a cold, wet and windy night. The memory of it sits with me still, like a half-cooked suet pudding.

After the bar closed there was nothing to do but sit it out, shivering and wondering if Robin had got my message and would be on hand to meet the boat. The problem, I knew, was that his body starts to function sometime around 10 AM and his mind about an hour later. The boat was due in at 7 AM. But the dawn came clear and cloudless and the sun popped up like a blood-red plate and the bar re-opened to serve that typical Spanish breakfast of black coffee laced with potent aniseed spirit. After a large 'breakfast', a sort of glow came upon me and I thought that perhaps he would indeed have roused himself against all his better inclinations.

Right on time, the great boat glided into Palma harbour – to a quay deserted save for a few taxi drivers, the odd docker, and a solitary figure that could only be Skelton's, pacing majestically up and down, occasionally shielding his eyes to scan the decks of the docking ferry. From the boat, he looked perfect. Not that the distance lent any especial enchantment, but perfect in that he was totally in character. His tan cotton summer suit was wrinkled beyond all description. His hands were thrust deep into his pockets, causing his trousers to ride up as if they had quarreled with his scuffed and tired-looking suede shoes. But none of this was in any way quite as remarkable as his hat. Robin has a passion for hats and not necessarily any old hat. This hat had passed well beyond the 'any old hat' point. Had he stolen it? If so, certainly not from any shop. This hat could only have been pinched from an unsuspecting donkey while its owner was selling cheap pottery to tourists. Had Skelton gone native? But native to where? If only he'd stuffed a half-finished bottle of wine into the pocket of that suit it would have been easy. Greene Land! Here was a living character from some Central American republic. *The Power and the Glory, Our Man in Havana* or *The Comedians*! He was looking for me, I assumed, but he ignored my waves and it was not until I strode down the gangplank that we really met.

By the time I was off the ship and we'd exchanged a few terse comments he'd decided it was breakfast time, so off we went in a cab up to the Plaza Gomilla. He makes it a habit while in Palma to wander down to this particular square each morning for his breakfast and to read the English papers. Over two or three Bloody Marys he scans the *Times* and, if the mood is on him, the *Guardian*. Showing a typical consideration, he had arranged for me to stay with a family which was to become a part of my life in the years to follow. The Kerrigans lived in a delightful old house in Terreno not far from the Plaza Gomilla, inhabited at one time by

Gertrude Stein and Alice Toklas. The whole building was full to overflowing with paintings, books, cats, plants, sculptures and children all trying to gain a little extra room.

Feeling quite genial after our 'breakfasts', we settled in and all the introductions were made. All but one. The smallest child, Malachay, was feeling a bit shy as he stood beside his mother, Elaine. He was dressed in a white suit and jacket held with a white sash which his mother explained was his karate outfit. In one of those perennially misguided ice-breaking moves, his mother asked the little lad if he would tell Robin what he had learned at the karate school. Whereupon the white-suited waif ran across the hall, gave out a loud scream and kicked the startled Skelton firmly on the kneecap. Having demonstrated his prowess, the boy backed off and turned to his mother with a broad smile on his face. That was what he had learned at karate school. We found a chair for Skelton, who was in shock, and also one for me as I was on the verge of hysteria. To this day Robin steers a wide circle around small boys in white suits and has placed them on his list of terrors in the same category as Airedale terriers. When calm settled, the problem of getting in touch with Robert Graves was addressed.

After a good deal of telephoning about by Elaine Kerrigan, we discovered that Robert Graves was not at home in Deya but in hospital right in Palma. It was arranged that we visit him there, for like all active men Graves was a terrible patient and he was sorely in need of a change in conversation. The three of us, Elaine Kerrigan, Robin and I, arrived at the clinic with me clutching two bottles of his favourite brand of very dry champagne.

We were ushered into his room and he and Robin went into a long discussion about writers they both knew and a good deal of character assassination followed. During a lull in the conversation, while they reloaded with fresh rounds of invective before the next batch of English poets faced their firing squad, I was ordered to open the wine. The fact that it was at a temperature consistent with the hot Spanish summer outside deterred no one. I found water glasses and set to work. The bottle did exactly as might have been predicted and the wine shot out like a hot spring. We were drenched – all of us, including the omnipresent crucifix on the wall above the bed. There was still enough wine to provide a sip all around and the conversation went on at full bore. Soon a second bottle was called for and I went off into the large tiled bathroom to try a second time. The cork exploded with a loud bang, but most of the wine was saved. I went back into the bedroom where the three of them were laughing their heads off. Graves had remarked to Skelton that I had really gone in there to shoot myself because of the disgrace of wasting all that good wine from the first bottle.

Graves was in hospital with a hernia, the result of his gardening vigour though he maintained his stay was to avoid some relations who were out from England for the summer. We left the clinic in a fine state, having arranged to return the following year to take part in Graves's 80th birthday celebrations for which Robin and I were to produce a special edition of *The Malahat Review*. It was one of those promises that was to come to a rare and wonderful fulfilment the following summer.

* * *

ONE OF THE MOST outstanding props in Professor Skelton's Travelling Medicine Show and Original Patented Snake Oil Extravaganza is his suitcase, and he won't leave home without it. It would be only mild hyperbole to call it elastic, for this wonderful bag has the capacity to expand and then expand again. Full, it looks much the same as a boa constrictor does after swallowing a couple of goats, horns and all. The bag is absolutely necessary for on the outward journey it is filled with sample copies of *The Malahat*, offprints, odd photographs and copies of books Robin has just finished writing or the manuscripts of books he is about to see published. A second bag is used for incidentals such as socks, booze and cigarettes. He travels light in the clothing department, offering the theory that if he took a lot of stuff he'd have to change and that might tire him out. The magical expanding suitcase never seems to grow any smaller for as fast as Robin dispenses books and gifts, so he is the recipient of books and manuscripts from others. On one occasion we had to get help to close the great bag. It took two of us standing on it to get the clasps close to the locks. Porters grew to hate that bag and it was a fine sight to see it and his others piled on a hand-cart, pushed by a sweating servant, with himself striding along behind, his straw hat on his head and his beard to the breeze, brandishing his stick at stray dogs on the way to the station.

The following year we were back again in Mallorca for Graves's birthday, but this time we had a specific task to perform.

The British Broadcasting Corporation had commissioned us to do a documentary on Robert Graves at 80. The whole affair was only possible because of the magic suitcase which was again taxed to capacity with studio-quality tape recorders, microphones and miles of blank tape. We were superbly equipped for the job, save for one vital component – Graves was only mildly interested. Robin did a valiant job each afternoon in the cool main room of Martin Tallent's house in Deya. We drank litres of Earl Grey tea and recorded miles of tape which at one point included a sort of community sing-song, despite Robin's aversion to singing. But the fact that the interviews ever produced anything is a tribute to Robin's persistence and the marvels of modern technology.

Tribute should also be paid to the reliability of the mini Seat which we hired to carry us and our stuff to Deya each afternoon. As is usual on such ventures we were on a budget that had been arrived at as a result of compromise. We could either get a decent car for a few days or an old, tiny car for as long as we liked. It was really no choice. We got this tiny car for a long time. But it may not have been such a saving, considering how long it took to get the stuff stowed away and Robin, bent like a paper clip, into the passenger seat. There he would sit, sweating like a grilling sausage, demanding to know how far it was to the next bar. Just before Deya there is a magnificent spring that cascades out of the mountain side, filling a cistern with ice-cold water from the depths of the earth. Here we would stop while he discarded his coat and plunged his arms into the cold water. I thought it must be putting disc brakes onto his heart beat but he survived the chill and went on to light his perennial cigarette and to demand more white wine.

The Graves birthday party was indeed a great success and so much so that the Guardia Civil sent men to direct the traffic. Robin was justly pleased with the special issue of *The Malahat Review* and was quite unable to meet demands for souvenir copies on the great day. It still seems odd in a way that the tributes to this greatest writer in English originated so far away, in a small town on the outermost edge of another continent. Graves loved it, for he was always a student of the anachronism. While in Mallorca we laid plans for the last special issue he was to oversee if not in fact edit. This was the tribute to Rafael Alberti that was honoured by Joan Miro with a special cover painted just for that issue. But for me, the Graves issue was the climax of Robin's career as editor-in-chief of *The Malahat Review*.

* * *

IN THE FOLLOWING YEARS our travels took us in different directions but again in 1978 we set off together on what was to prove a comic progression. Robin is not in any way addicted to sporting events but he is a perennial student of people. This was the year of World Cup Soccer, and we were ordained to follow it in three or four countries. But first there was a major problem to settle and it came to a head after we had left for London from Cambridge University, where we stayed and were feasted at high table in St. John's College. It came about this way. London is a terrible place to be in search of rooms during the summer season when every academic in the known and unknown universe is working on something in the British Library. The reading room looks for all the world like a penal colony as row upon row of blue and white striped suits occupy the seats, heads down in some intent act of academic penal servitude.

We managed by dint of good deal of phoning and mucking about to find a room at Mrs. Nitwell's Guest and Academic Retreat somewhere in West Kensington. The room itself had a sort of entrance hall and then a large bedroom with two beds that had seen better days in an army camp. Skelton, claiming seniority and rank – I think he was a corporal or acting sergeant in the Royal Air Force – got the bed by the window. After all this time I have grown immune to his aversion to any form of water that is not an ice cube in a tall glass of Irish, but there was also now the matter of his noise. He can be very, very noisy.

He starts to snore at 1 AM on the dot and slowly builds to a crescendo by about 2 AM when all rational thought ceases. I have tried all forms of counter-measure including drinking large amounts of whisky. The result of this last was only that I had to endure his ursine rumblings with a hangover. In the end I took a more drastic step. I lugged all my bedding into the tiny ante-room and set the tape recorder going at his bedside. By stuffing my ears with the cotton out of the top of an aspirin bottle and putting a pillow over my head, I got to sleep.

Great indeed was his chagrin in the morning when he found I had gone and equally great was his relief when he found that it was only around the corner. The matter of the tape was quite another thing. I outlined the problem to him in as quiet and controlled a manner as I could muster and then I played the tape back to him. It is hard to visualize him speechless but on this occasion it happened. He just could not believe that the dreadful rumblings and snorts punctuated by vile growls were in any way connected with himself. For perhaps only a moment he looked devastated and contrite.

The humility was not to last, for by the time we reached our next destination, back at Cambridge, he was in his old, full form.

We dined at a number of the colleges and Robin thoroughly enjoyed ruffling a few feathers over the port and Stilton, but soon we got tired of it all and set off for France.

Despite his interest in art and the pleasure he takes in visiting galleries, Robin has little enthusiasm for Paris. We were there only long enough to change trains and sink a few glasses before we were on our way to Macon. It was a delightful stopover marred only by the great man's getting stuck in the lavatory. We were in a small hotel room over a bar and the facilities were of the more primitive type, to be found down the hall, on a tiny landing. They were never designed for the Skeltonic bulk and he found it a mite cramped. His problems were compounded by the fact that the door opened outwards onto the landing which was in total darkness. The light could only be activated by pushing one of those timer buttons which put on the light for about 30 seconds and then off it goes again. The button was outside the toilet. Wondering what had happened to him during a lengthy absence that night, I set off to the landing and found the light. He emerged after some time with his Francophobia fully restored. The dark, cramped, smelly lavatory had confirmed all his secret fears about France.

We carried on south by train. Our stops in Marseilles and Barcelona were pleasant – Barcelona especially so, as we enjoyed an excellent gossipy lunch with Robert Graves's daughter Lucia and her husband Ramon. All the time we kept touch with the World Cup Soccer action on television. From Barcelona we returned to France to visit Carcassonne. Following our tried and true formula we parked our cases in railway lockers and looked about. After an excellent lunch, Robin insisted on walking all over the old walled city, which disposed of the afternoon. He'd timed it so that we would be back in a bar in time to watch the soccer. Normally he doesn't watch a sporting event on the box from one year's end to the next but, as the Victorians said, travel seems to broaden the mind.

In the early evening we got into a bar full of paratroopers who were on a training exercise. We got to talking about tattoos with them and soon it was shirts off and drinks all round. By the time we got to dinner we were in fine condition but enjoyed large plates of cassoulet and more wine. It was following this that Robin decided to change his clothes and so we set off back to the station. On arrival, he took out his ever-expanding case from the locker and to my amazement and amusement he proceeded to get undressed in the station concourse while at the same time rummaging about for fresh clothes. There he was, down to his briefs, holding up two rumpled shirts and trying to decide which one to wear. There was a definite raising of gallic eyebrows at the station. Having dressed and put his stuff away he decided it was time for a nap. Outside the station there was a small pond and a grassy bank so he went no further. Down he crashed and just before he dropped off to sleep he mumbled that I was to wake him if anything interesting happened or I had any bright ideas on where to go next.

After strolling about town I found myself back at the station where Skelton was still terrifying the ducks with his snores and rumblings. In the station hall there was a large board that announced the arrival of trains and their destinations. It said that in 15 minutes the express from Madrid to Rome would make a short stop. Somehow I got Robin awake and told him we were off to Rome right away and he had to get his act together. He struggled into action and we got our last bag into a compartment just as the train began to move. I recall we slept most of the way with occasional breaks for salami sandwiches and beer.

We arrived in Rome late in the evening and as we had no hotel booked there was the problem of lodgings. One of the few bright things we have devised is a method of finding rooms. Robin finds a decent bar in the general area of where we want to stay and then after a couple of restoratives I leave him with the bags while I wander about checking out the hotels. In Rome we were really lucky for we found excellent accommodations just across the street from old friends who are resident in Rome. I have spent quite a number of weeks in Rome and have yet to set foot in a museum but Robin had a small list of things he had to see and so we occupied our time in different ways.

Each evening there seemed to be a new celebration going on at our friends' house. We had a large party to celebrate our arrival in Rome, then it was the birthday of my friend's mother. Then I cooked dinner for 30 people. Following that, an Italian friend said we had never had good chicken until we had tried those from the countryside around Rome. He shut up his business for the day and went off in his truck to find the right birds.

Robin volunteered to help with the chickens and was given the job of cutting them up. He didn't know, and nobody told him, that the birds had not been cleaned inside. Soon he was surrounded by yards of chicken entrails and odd as it may seem, thoroughly enjoying himself. That party sticks out in my memory as being a good one, for on top of the cooking, Robin was also moved to song. This act resembles his approach to foreign languages – the less he knows about it the louder he shouts. But sing he did and got a good hand for his efforts.

It was soon after this that we had to part company as I had appointments to keep in London. We enjoyed a number of visits with the Spanish writer and artist Rafael Alberti and organized material for that issue of *The Malahat Review* and then I had to leave. The night before, we met in a bar for a drink and Robin wanted to try the local grappa. It was another good evening and I left him the following morning with his notes on what he wanted to visit that day. We arranged to meet in London before setting out for home.

Robin is the best of travelling companions for he seldom gets ruffled and is always content to go his own way for a few days if the mood suits him. Best of all, he never loses his sense of humour even under the most trying circumstances.

I still wonder if a particular customs officer at Vancouver Airport has a sense of humour. He asked Robin to open the magical, ever-expanding suitcase. We had arrived back on a blistering hot day and the room was crowded. Robin did as he was asked. The effect was dramatic. He had jammed the top of his case with all his old socks and underwear. Totally unwashed, they had reached the point of fermentation. It was as if a blue cheese had been left in the sun for a month. The horrified customs man took a step backwards, a tortured look on his face. He said not a word but waved us on. The Professor Skelton Travelling Medicine Show and Patented Snake Oil Extravaganza was home.

'Nymph and Neptune', woodcut 1981 by Herbert Siebner RCA.

Moncrieff Williamson
Robin and the UFO

MY COPY OF TIMELIGHT by my fellow Limner notes in tidy
handwriting that it is 'inscribed for Crieff with gratitude and
friendship on the occasion of my first visit to Prince Edward
Island. Robin. February 1975.'

The weather was true to its February threat of being the worst:
gales, blizzards, sub-zero (Fahrenheit in those days), and just the
weather to keep an audience for poetry readings at home. Robin
Skelton, fine poet and creator of exquisite collages, read in ringing
tones his admirable verse. Roses in Victoria, snow-covered thorns
in PEI. That time of year.

As always, Robin was generous with his time, talked wisely and
gave no indication that inwardly he faced a crisis. Having come
this far from his British Columbia territory, he had chosen to
spend an additional day for visiting Confederation Centre with the
understanding that he must leave on the third morning. He was
due back in Victoria to welcome officially a distinguished guest-
lecturer, a Fellow from Cambridge University. It looked now that
he might be storm-stayed in Charlottetown for a further forty-
eight hours.

A further obstacle. While Robin's plane was due to depart from
Moncton, New Brunswick, at approximately 11 AM, a strike by
snow-shovellers and snow-removal employees meant that all
airports in Atlantic Canada were closed. Except Moncton, kept
open by some Federal regulation that provided emergency landings
for transatlantic flights. Moncton was obligated to remain open
365 days a year, strikes or not.

Problem. The distance between Charlottetown and Moncton in
those days was 91 miles. (When we switched to metric, this
became 148 kilometres. As our PEI information service reassured
Islanders in print, the distance remained the same.) So an early

start meant early to bed if we were to catch the first ferry crossing. I warned our guest that sometimes ferries are cancelled. Poor visiting professor from England. Poor Robin, so far from the flower gardens of Oak Bay.

So for Robin's final evening in Charlottetown my wife Pam cooked the finest of foods and Robin and I enjoyed several glasses of malt and a bottle or so of wine. We discussed all aspects of Canadian literary activities and in the customary way so well-suited to our vast land, kept each other up to date with regional gossip. Then the telephone. 9:30 PM.

My friend, Dr. Ian Stewart, then Head of Psychiatry for PEI hospitals, telephoning to let Pam and me know that outside his house on Brighton Road a crowd had assembled to look at an Unknown Flying Object. He suggested we should hurry if we wished to see this unusual sight. Pam decided it was too cold.

Brighton Road runs alongside Victoria Park and ends at a 'T' intersection about five blocks from our house. To the left, the harbour-side road is blocked with mammoth snow drifts. To the right, where residents live in executive-style Tudor, the road is kept clear. People were arriving in excited groups. Because it was so cold we chomped our winter boots and flapped our arms and stared at the clear, star-dotted sky.

High over the farming district of York Point, across the stretch of water where the North River enters our harbour bay, was the Flying Object. Only it wasn't flying. It was stationary. A brilliantly shining disc; a giant earth-station TV satellite receiver, only it wasn't. It had the light-intensity of a searchlight.

I haven't the mathematical nor engineering skills for estimating heights or trajectories. My intuitive guess placed this brilliant circle at a height of between 80 to 150 feet, at a distance of three-quarters of a mile from our road. From the time it had been first spotted to the sudden black-out, as if the White Goddess or some other poet's Muse had switched off the light, our UFO was visible for a period of fifteen minutes.

There have been other mysterious objects and optical illusions recorded in our local press, but nothing comparable and seen by so many observers at the same time. (The latest was this winter, a tracker aircraft on night exercises from Summerside CFB.) So it was not early bed. It was late talk. And puzzlement.

The ferry, as anticipated, was a slow journey between ice blocks. Without ice-breaking prow and equipment it would have been impossible to cross the 9 mile strait. This, together with the UFO, was almost too much for Robin.

'Have you a camera?' he pleaded. 'Nobody in Victoria will ever believe me when I tell them I've been in the Arctic Circle! I must have proof!' So I took snapshots of Robin Skelton, Arctic explorer. The drive from Cape Tormentine to Moncton airport called on all my skill as a winterized driver, but we made it, just as Robin's plane was coming in to land. In the twenty-five years I've known him, this was the only time I've seen him hurry.

I wonder if, at the advanced age of 60, Robin still believes in UFOs? You should ask him. I know that I do. But then, as the Irish – which I'm not – might say, I've had eight more years than he has. In age and friendship, distances are the same. It is good to reminisce about the improbable.

Fleur Adcock
Coast to Coast

I. WEST

III

'From shore to shining shore.'
Or, as we now say, coast to coast:
from coast to bleeding coast and back again
in fourteen days. Three British poets,
jet-lagged already, and it's only Sunday;
and this is Victoria, BC.

'You'll like Victoria, it's so English,'
English? We can have that at home:
we've just flown over the Rockies, we want
grain-hoppers and grizzly bears.
Lead us to your trackless forests,
your endless prairies under snow,

your lumberjacks and fur-trappers.
When shall we need snowshoes? Give us
cliches!
        The afternoon is mild,
sunny and gentle. We've been driven
along the Summit Trail to a rocky knoll
which could be in the Lake District –

apart from the madrona tree,
its ragged wrapping-paper bark, its
foreign berries. Thank you; and yes,
we liked the little oaks. And of course the view:
enough to make us all light-headed,
which in any case we were already.

*

No, it's not English. But it has devices
to make us feel at home – or to make me,
at least, see in its colonial bungalows
leafed off by trees a recognisable suburb
(of Auckland, I'd say, flicking through comparisons
in the back files on my other country.)

Who's English, anyway? Not you, now, Robin,
ex-Yorkshireman, Canadian citizen,
on your home ground here as I've never seen you:
frail suddenly, thinner, unexpectedly limping
but flourishing that silver-headed cane
like an accessory you'd always wanted –

a foil for your flashy rings. You're undiminished:
the chuckles gurgle through your beard,
the stories flow. It's your island we're
seeing bits of on the way from the airport,
your crew-cut son at the wheel; and now he's brought us
through farmland (kale and cattle) to

the sea. The Sea. 'Thalassa!' I want to shout,
silly with salt air. Look, the Pacific!
Cormorants diving into it, great logs
of driftwood, grey-green swell slapping the pebbles.
I shall stand here on the shining shore
and nothing will get me back into the car.

                             *

The meal they took us to before the reading was
Japanese (Japan's just over there,
separated from this island by nothing
but ocean and the guillotined edge of
the page in any atlas you consult
where the Pacific's not left whole.)

Hot mounds of threatening crab! Indelicate
delicacy, pronged with claws and shell-shards:
unmanageable. But not to us, who are
learning to manage, disciplined as we are
by schedules and itineraries,
by Arlene's motherly hands (purveyors

of cheques and lists and airline tickets
and hotel reservations) back in Toronto
where it's 3 AM, the time our stomachs tell –
unless they say it's London, 8 AM,
breakfast-time. Here it's midnight now,
and this is the after-the-reading party,

in P.K. Page's house, elegant as
herself and her poems. She's given me
her latest book; and Robin's given me
his; and Dorothy Livesay's given me ...
Are they all poets here? Mike's one of them:
we've known each other twenty-seven years,

from Wellington; tonight we squatted on
the stairs together for perhaps ten minutes.
I think he asked me 'What's it all about?'
I think I laughed.
                Back to the party.
A poet admires my necklace: Pacific
pearl-shell, from the Cook Islands,

a gift. And they ask where we go next:
Vancouver tomorrow, Tuesday Edmonton,
Wednesday Saskatoon ... P.K.'s made coffee.
Victoria's not Canada, she says: It's
a nice place, but nothing to do with my country.'
I shan't find out what it has to do with mine.

W.D. Valgardson
Meeting Robin Skelton

THE FIRST TIME I heard from Robin Skelton, I was in Nevada, Missouri. The phone rang and his enthusiastic, hearty English voice offered to take me away from the evils of America and back into the safe and sane bosom of Canada.

'Come teach at the University of Victoria,' he said.

Years before, I'd been to visit my wife's grandmother in Victoria. Lake most Victorians, she was a stubble-jumper who had got tired of winter. I remembered market gardens, cherry trees, monkey-puzzle trees, the ivy-covered Empress, the rich aroma of Murchie's spice and tea emporium, but not a university. What, I wondered, would the newly wed and the nearly dead want with a university?

'You want me to teach in the English Department?' I asked.

'Creative Writing Department,' he replied with some feeling. 'I want you to teach fiction.'

Creative Writing is as American as Mom and Apple Pie. They invented it. They nurtured it. In Canada it was regarded with the same contempt as underwater basket-weaving.

What, I wondered, was an Englishman (Englishmen are even bigger academic snobs than Canadians) doing running a creative writing department in that most unlikely of places, a Canadian university? Whoever Robin Skelton was, I decided, he must be an extraordinary Englishman to buck so much tradition.

I told Robin that I already had accepted a job at a Baptist University in Texas. But those of you who know Robin know that once he's decided on something, trying to resist is like beating the sea with chains to keep the tide from coming in. Before the call was over, I agreed to throw over a life in the sun, my weekend dreams of a cottage on the Gulf of Mexico, and move to the land of rain and retirement.

The trip – with a wife, two kids, a cat, and the largest U-haul trailer in the world, a trailer crammed with everything from plants to a piano – was a nightmare. The car overheated in Kansas, the fan belt broke in Colorado, the overloaded trailer nearly pulled us off a steep mountain road (in Utah, I think) but, finally, after five days, there we were in Port Angeles, eating steamed clams. Canada was a dim line on the horizon.

In Victoria, tired, irritable, we searched for our house. When we found it, it was much nicer than we expected. Everything had been arranged by mail. The owner, before he left for Europe for a year, had mailed us the front door key. Then, being a careful, meticulous person, locked all the doors and windows and set the deadbolt on the front door. I entered my new home through a window which I'd broken with a rock. What, I thought, if we've got the address wrong? I'll go to jail for a B and E.

The next day I had lunch with Robin.

I should mention that I'm virtually a teetotaler, dreadfully conservative, and had just come from teaching for four years at a private women's college / finishing school where I spent a lot of time at formal receptions sipping pink lemonade. The year I left, 1974, the young women still had formal teas, wore white gloves and learned how to be wives for successful businessmen. The born-again conservatism can be suggested by the fact that the kitchen staff deliberately burned four hundred meals because the chef had included burgundy in the recipe.

I never truly understood the word antithesis until, coming from this environment, I met Robin. What I remember, eleven years later, is long hair and beard, large rings, a vortex of noise, laughter, endless people stopping at the table to swap stories, and Irish whisky. I drank lunch. We may have eaten something but, if so, I don't remember it. I think I laughed a lot. After lunch, Robin, none the worse for wear, sped away to run the department, write another book and teach classes with the undiminished energy of a Missouri tornado.

My new house was only five blocks away from campus but it took me two hours to find it. At last, I struggled up the stairs and, to my startled wife, said, 'Ate too much' before collapsing on our bed.

Later, recovering over a pot of coffee, I made a prophecy. 'Teaching with Robin,' I said, 'isn't going to be like teaching with the Baptists.'

Robert O'Driscoll
O Lord, Deliver us

for RS with memories of his poem 'The Rake'

'From this scourge of rakes,
    this exposer of fakes,
    this dredger of lakes,
      O Lord Deliver us.

'From this scythe of bad art,
    this upsetter of carts,
    this mocker of Sartre,
      O Lord deliver us.'

So pray his enemies,
Of whom there are many, as
Our bold man Robin
Is a ceaseless bobbin,
A fierce-eyed falcon:
    'From the ire of Skelton.'
    They cringe, they cry,
    'O good Lord deliver us,
    Deliver us, we pray.'

II

But his friends on the other side
Rise up and say: 'His heart is wide
As a mountain, and deep as the sea,
    And that heart
    Has served true art
    Of man and woman.'

So, we, of the tribe of Robin,
Warmed in the fire of Skelton,
    Unite in proclaiming him
    Our father pelican.
May he work till four score,
May he live for even more.
Good Lord, deliver him, we pray,
From breath of disease and sign of decay.

Charles Lillard
Victoria Avenue's Open Door

WHEN ASKED A SHORT TIME AGO to write briefly about Robin
Skelton's years in British Columbia, his work with the Creative
Writing Department at the University of Victoria, and his
subsequent work with the Sono Nis Press, I agreed happily. Now,
several attempts later, I doubt whether the story can be told
briefly, or even accurately. Robin has done too much and,
inadvertently or not, he has stepped on too many toes. Many old
fogeys still see him as a British upstart: 'He couldn't make it at
home so he came out here to the colonies.' Any number of younger
men and women call Robin 'cunning and devious', 'an empire
builder', 'dictatorial' and 'dangerous'. In few places can one find
three people out of four who agree about Robin Skelton. And
there is also the legendary Robin, the man who writes books with
the ease others write letters, the bibliophile, the artist and
collector, the magician. Here truth and fiction are so intertwined
that working out the details will surely one day become a graduate
school industry. My only alternative is to write of the man and his
time from my own angle, and while such a view may be cranky at
moments, that is part of the pleasure of writing about a friend,
ally, and teacher.

* * *

ROBIN HAD SET the interview at ten. Previously this had seemed the
perfect time to meet Robin; now, parked in front of his home, it
was all wrong – I was totally unprepared. Would I get the job?
And if Robin did hire me, did I really want to work for him?
Teaching in the University of Victoria's Creative Writing
Department sounded fine on paper, but ...
    This was the late spring of 1974. Like most of the people I
knew in Vancouver, which had been home for most of the
previous eight winters, I found it hard to take Victoria seriously.
For one thing, the town was widely known as being a humourless
rumour-mill, where the purpose of gossip was not entertainment,
but spite. Insofar as a cultural community existed there at all, it
seemed a bitter one, ruled by writers and artists who had been
considered major, prior to the cultural revolution that shook
British Columbia in the late 1960s, and whose survival was now
mean-spirited at best. Every one of them know that Modernism

was a conspiracy. Most of it, they would corner one to insist, was mental vomit. One Victoria *Colonist* writer was not content to merely deprecate the work of one of Canada's youngest poets (and he had already disparaged the work of every poet since Tennyson in his non-stop rant), he went on to libel her in such a way that his comments cannot be repeated outside a court of law. This outburst came at the end of an otherwise sane telephone conversation, but what made it even more remarkable was that the newspaperman was a total stranger to me.

This fringe group was not all that was on my mind as I paced Robin's sidewalk. Worse, that spring morning, for a writer toying with teaching creative writing, was the lack of serious contemporaries in Victoria. True, Robin, Derk Wynand, and Lawrence Russell were in the department at the University of Victoria. It was rumoured that P.K. Page lived somewhere nearby, but as she had published only one completely new book in the past twenty years, she was looked upon by most of my generation as a relic from the past. Robert Sward, only three or four years earlier one of the few internationally-known poets in Canada, had become a local guru. And the younger writers (Susan Musgrave, Marilyn Bowering, Seán Virgo) who had gathered around Robin were now elsewhere. A few academic writers and poets were known to be teaching in the university's English department, and while I had read their work while editing (with J. Michael Yates and George McWhirter) the original manuscript of *Contemporary Poetry of British Columbia,* if they had written anything new, word of this had not reached the BC mainland. The only literary magazine in Victoria was *The Malahat Review,* edited by Skelton. By comparison with Vancouver's creative mêlée, its magazines and publishing houses, this community looked lean and desperate.

Finally, there was the problem of Robin Skelton himself. If one believed the rumours, the man was a Rabelaisian Tennyson or worse. Similar rumours circulated about J. Michael Yates, but Yates was a friend and 'wild man' though he might have been in some circumstances, I knew he could not live up to 75 per cent of his reputation. Although I had never worked with Robin, I knew his work, our trails had crossed numerous times since 1968, and I suspected the truth-fiction ratio in Skelton's case would prove about the same as Yates's. But a recurring theme in those rumours held that Skelton's major interest in life was in building his own reputation. Did I care to work for and with such an ego? I was not at all sure that I did.

Considering my bleak view that morning, it surprises me today that I reached his home, much less got out of my car to pace the street. But I know why I was there. There were two reasons, and one of them was curiosity. I wanted to know how Robin managed to teach and write. The latter I knew he did well, and former students praised his lectures and seminars. None of the teaching writers I knew in Vancouver or Toronto controlled this balance. My view was élitist – a man or woman who produces a book every five or six years is a hobbyist. One of the fads of the period was to join the labour force; senseless work would, it was reasoned, give a writer the mental space to create. Well, I had been there before the fad began, and I knew the difficulties involved. Robin appeared to have found a niche and a method, but what was it?

The other reason was the Creative Writing Department. It was, from all I had heard, the only viable department of its kind in Canada. Graduates walked out of its doors into the literary marketplace. The Creative Writing Department at the University of British Columbia functioned as a pasture for tenured hobbyists (with the notable exceptions of Robert Harlow and George McWhirter). Other Canadian writing programmes worked in those days (usually in scattered attic lumber rooms above English departments) on the American academic theory: writing was something one did in spare moments. Only Robin's department was a trade school where young poets and fiction writers were also taught the more general skills of the literary world.

When it came, the interview was brief and to the point. There was none of the glad-handing, dithering and double-talk so common to academic and professional interviews. Robin Skelton had questions; he wanted my answers; in conclusion, he told me what he expected. Sitting there, thinking of Robin's reputation and pleased with his direct approach, I could not help but think of two other men whose reputations were equally monstrous, and who interviewed in a similar manner – Dave Murdey and Steve Zablosky, two woods bosses of the old school. Both operated with one simple rule: they told you what to do, and if you did not do it immediately and to the best of your ability, they fired you. They expected total loyalty and gave a loyalty in return that is all but inexplicable in today's world of unions and committees. Everything about Robin that morning suggested he operated with the same rule. This made me feel a great deal better; such men are easy to work for and with. When I left a few minutes later, with one last lusting glance at the books in the room, I knew the job was mine. And I knew I wanted it. Writing and publishing were as important as teaching; community teaching, reading, exchange lectures – all were to be considered part of my job. There would be no lily-fingered poets in this atmosphere.

Although I knew Victoria's cultural atmosphere was rank, how fetid it truly was came as a shock. Complaining and back-biting were endemic: if it was not the weather that was bad it was the city, if not the students, the administration. With the exception of Rosemary Sullivan, Doug Beardsley, and Robin Skelton, no one I met in the literary / cultural community those first few months was able to say anything decent about the University of Victoria. Doug and Rosemary, just back from almost a decade in England and Europe, were too busy with their own work to gripe and snipe. So was Robin.

Skelton was running the department and doing it, so far as I could tell, with little help or input from anyone on his staff. He was editing *The Malahat Review,* sitting on various committees, doing an enormous amount of writing, and teaching his full load of classes. Even lunch at the Faculty Club seemed to give him no respite, had he wanted it. Lunch for Robin was wine and a good meal and work. If it was not departmental business, it was entertaining visitors. There was always time to help people sort out administrative problems, work out details for tenure and promotion, agree to read manuscripts, discuss publishers. Of the dozens of meals we shared that first year or so, I can recall few that were not interrupted by someone joining us to ask a favour of Robin.

That many of those people who asked favours would not have bothered to throw Robin a rope if he were drowning did not seem to matter to him, if he was aware of the situation. I was and it did annoy me. Yet I was in no position to speak aloud of any of this. At the time, I thought he was aware of what was going on, for it certainly was not limited to him alone. Few of my colleagues had anything worthwhile to say about one another privately, though most were quite friendly socially.

But as I have never heard Robin say anything totally negative about anyone at the University of Victoria (or anywhere else for that matter), I'm forced to conclude that he either did not know of this animosity, or thought it part of the wide-spread reluctance to believe that a creative writing department could be functional and might be necessary. Often this 'reluctance' amounted to contempt on campus and off, and it was not alleviated by the department's growing track record. In 1974-1975 the classes were filled to overflowing, several of us taught classes at night, and the courses we developed for the university's Extension Programme were popular and full. This annoyed the critics. Then Robin had the audacity to bring in American and British writers as visiting lecturers – 'most of them personal friends', ran the critical refrain. There was no end to the complaining; to sort it out today would be as boring as it would be pointless. That year, like Robin's career at the University of Victoria, could best be summed up as having been marred by success.

During 1974-1975 gossiping and back-biting at the university reached epidemic proportions. The summer of 1975 did nothing to dispel the atmosphere and Robin, according to rumour, had grown even more autocratic and demanding. Everything I learned was second-hand; I doubt I saw Robin or anyone else from the department a half-dozen times between May and September. Yet when I began seeing him daily during registration week, I found Robin unchanged. What had changed was the attitude of the full-time members of his staff. The complaining had localized: Robin was dictatorial; he was moving too fast. This thinking grew until one of the staff wrote a letter to the Dean, complaining of Robin's behaviour. It has been said that this pulled the proverbial rug from beneath Robin's feet. He did resign his position as Head of the Creative Writing Department, but this was his decision, no one else's. Robin knew that the head of a young and small department cannot function properly if his full-time staff fails to be supportive.

And the rest was anti-climactic. Robin went home, sick and tired, and stayed there, writing and reading, until the next fall term began. An acting-head was appointed from outside the department, and one had to be watching a particular face in the departmental meeting where this appointment was announced to appreciate the black humour in this administrative move. It had obviously not been considered in a certain game plan. Older students complained, and not all all quietly, that they were getting the short end of the stick; Robin was the only full-time member, they felt, who had the experience to give them their money's worth. Stupidly, I took over most of Robin's teaching load – 'stupidly' because more than one person warned me that the university would fail to pay me for this work. More curious, from my position, was the acting-head's attempt to keep the record of this 21-hour teaching load off my university curriculum vitae. Someone upstairs wanted to forget the entire pointless episode in the Creative Writing Department. Whether or not that letter and Robin's subsequent action had any long-range effect on the department is still a topic of many late night discussions. Speculation is always fun, and it's a game in which everyone can take an active part. Personally, all that I'm sure of is that the department retreated into the university to such an extent that it has been largely forgotten by the cultural community in Victoria and, so far as I can tell, this ignorance extends to Vancouver and points north and east. However, one of the immediate reactions to Robin's resignation was a clearing of the atmosphere. The letter-writer's motives were so unclear, his behind-the-back attack so despicable, the results so negligible, almost immediately people began to realize the realize the dangers in pointless complaining. Another result was a shift in opinion in Robin's favour. Many felt that the administration's handling of the affair had been shabby at best; wasn't Robin one of the University's only major drawing cards, it was reasoned, hadn't he single-handedly created the Creative Writing Department, hadn't he been instrumental in creating the Special Collections Room, and was it not Robin who had made *The Malahat Review* an internationally known magazine? Off-campus the response was more remarkable. People remembered that it was Robin, and no one else, who had set up an evening programme for young writers; he had written art criticism for a local newspaper at a time when no one else would and – they remembered suddenly how much else he had done within the community. One can almost underline the spring of 1976 as the date when the local, and much of the national, bitching about Robin the Foreigner stopped dead in its tracks.

During the spring term, I began visiting Robin at home, partially due to class and *Malahat* business, but largely because I missed our conversations. Of all the local writers he was a man of letters in the healthy and traditional sense, and I had found Robin's unbuttoned manner and inexhaustible fund of ideas refreshing. At his home I met a Robin whom I had only glimpsed previously. Here was the family man. Three children were at home in that large and endlessly interesting house. Robin's elderly mother had only recently moved from England to live with her son; as well, his mother- and father-in-law were often visiting; there seemed to be always one or two newcomers staying in spare rooms, and the children's friends roamed everywhere. Robin's wife, Sylvia, seemed continually involved in four or five projects that she appeared to manage perfectly. The children, the radios, stereos and television, phones ringing and visitors like myself coming and going. What a ménage!

The front door was open to everyone. If Victoria had an artistic-literary centre that spring it was in Skelton's living-room. In the middle of all this activity sat Robin, drink in hand, carrying on several conversations at once, his mind teeming with projects. People who did not visit him during this period have since claimed he sat at home 'licking his wounds'. Nothing could be further from the truth. Certainly he was hurt by that stab in the dark by a colleague, yet he seemed to know better than anyone else that being head of a department is a dubious honour, and that the work outweighs the supposed glory. Personally I was delighted to know he was now free to begin the various jobs I watched him sketch out in his ever-present notebook.

The most important event of the next few months was not one we had discussed. We could not have foreseen that J. Michael Yates would turn over the Sono Nis Press to Charles and Richard Morriss. This happened while Robin and Sylvia were vacationing in Oregon. In response to Dick Morriss's phone call, Robin agreed to become editor.

Mike Yates started Sono Nis in 1968 to answer the demand for a quality literary press in western Canada. Although it had published the first work of Wynand, Bringhurst, Musgrave, Schroeder, Virgo, Lawrence Russell, and Marilyn Bowering, as well as later books by Rona Murray, George Amabile, Robert Harlow, Robin Skelton, and Robert Zend, in 1976 it was known mainly as a literary press with a contentious nature. What is too often overlooked is that this reputation was not based on the people published; it was a result of Yates's own cantankerous personality. This, distribution problems, the press's ever-changing address, and the prevailing theory that if a press was not sanctioned by George Woodcock it could not possibly be of value, had done irreparable damage to Yates's original idea.

In those first editorial meetings of the new Sono Nis board, a number of cures were discussed. The very name (a Gaelic-Italian combination meaning I am / I am not) came under scrutiny. From the first, Robin insisted the press needed a philosophy and a shape. He knew Sono Nis could never compete with the major Canadian publishing houses at the distribution or publicity levels, yet with hard work it could be revitalized and again become what Yates originally created: a quality literary press. And by widening its horizons Sono Nis could become the major British Columbia publishing house.

Robin Skelton, with the solid backing of the Morrisses, accomplished all he set out to do in what now seems a remarkably short time. Almost immediately the press began publishing local history, history, art, poetry and fiction – books which while having a major local audience, also appealed to a larger and more general readership. This was the 'shape' or publishing policy Robin knew to be a necessity.

This publishing philosophy was more English than North American. He wanted to continue publishing the authors Yates had begun publishing, to publish quality first collections of poetry and prose, and despite the lack of public interest to publish the best work available in those categories. Better than anyone else at those early editorial meetings, Robin knew a house must create its audience.

One way to measure the success of Robin's thinking as editor is to look at the competition in British Columbia. The once well-known Hancock House has almost disappeared; Gray's Publishing appears to exist in name only; Talonbooks and the University of British Columbia Press publish spasmodically; Oolichan Books is a carbon copy of the Sono Nis literary arm; Douglas & McIntyre publishes books of Canadian interest, distributes American and British books, and is turning to educational publishing. Alone in British Columbia Sono Nis has a steadily growing list of books by Canadians for Canadians.

Distribution is the problem even Robin Skelton's work and vision as an editor could not overcome. If this is a black mark, and some claim so, it is shared by other publishers. The majority of books nominated for the Governor General's Award in 1983 and 1984 did not reach Victoria book stores within the calendar year of publication; many did not even reach reviewers before the awards were announced. Distribution is a Canadian problem. In this country distribution only works when books are remaindered. Robin Skelton and Dick Morriss have never allowed Sono Nis to remainder its books.

* * *

WRITING IN *The Malahat Review* in the spring of 1978, I suggested that George Woodcock, J. Michael Yates, and Robin Skelton were largely responsible for the cultural upheaval in British Columbia between 1966 and 1972. George Woodcock's role as a public voice continues to grow, although his authority as a judge of contemporary poetics is questionable. He belongs to the generation led by the spell of Auden. Few of these writers made the transition from their origins to late twentieth-century poetics as easily as they made the step from poetry to prose. Yates's importance as a teacher and innovator does not seem to have survived the 1970s. And Robin Skelton, thirteen years younger than Woodcock and thirteen older than Yates, remains as creative, influential and young as he was when I made that statement.

Robin, as a creator and touchstone in Victoria, is not just a case of a big fish in a little pond. While his youthful zest is basically an inherent quality, the amount of work he produces and his absolute genuineness as a person are to some extent a result of his living in Victoria. A city without a culture, as Thomas Mann suggested of Munich, is the best of all places to live and write. There can be no serious distractions. Here, if one chooses to remain, one must create his or her own creative atmosphere. No one has done this so successfully and to the same extent as has Robin, and the benefits are becoming increasingly obvious. Other writers his age are becoming public figures and public voices, some are drinking themselves into oblivion, and many are scratching hard ground in hopes of surviving as artists. Robin Skelton lives quietly in Victoria, having created the ultimate writer's world – one which revolves around him in a city incapable of understanding culture unless it is spelled out with dollar signs. And he teaches at a university that pays him one of the highest salaries paid to a Canadian professor. The system is licking his boots. Although he never has said a word about it to me, I suspect Robin knew something like this lay in the future when he arrived in Victoria in 1962. The man is always in control, and he's a man who is always a jump or two ahead of the rest of us.

Luella Kerr
1255 Victoria Avenue

to Robin Skelton

A romantic house
wears its family easily,
graces space, outside and in
by use: is welcoming.

A devon cream invitation
on a dark night, many windows lit
to travel a rose-petalled path,
past a coaching lamp
up broad front steps:
is sincere as trees.

Has shade for any fretful summer,
rooms of belles-lettres' manners
shelves and walls affectionate
to art, wintered knobs
secret nooks innocent as spring,
a nave witched as history:
is wise.

Glossed paper-white and black,
in daylight, large and solid
on its corner lot
garden casual from caring,
it sticks out a tongue
of chimney brick, copies
the sure, mad smile of autumn,
ignores two large viridian fingers
admonishing from the gate:
is good but daring.

A romantic house is any shape,
or size, or kind – of home:
is lyric stimulation for the heart,
and ah:

is heroic.

Chad Evans
Mr. Skelton Incognita

The Celtic albatross predates
navigation by stars, leaning to current
off Iceland, Greenland and performs
a sea-dance pursued by Norsemen.

It lands and mates every three years
before it dies, sighting outcrops,
Pacific cordillera, *Nouvelle Hollande,*
Odysseus in a dreamtime of rocks.

Inland transmontane fringes cliffside
like colonies are established
through prosody and song, spells
crafting petroglyphs, arcadian views.

British Columbia seemed a university
of the sky, this albatross alighting
below the gloaming of imaginative clouds
supernatural raincoast of a prehistoric numen.

Familial flights to the Cariboo
fossicking gold rush myths all summer
he wintered on an island grove of Academe,
London calling only as a footnote.

Administrative, editorial years yawned
while frontier progeny were nestled
amid a West Coast school of intuition,
a gaggle of Gaelic liars untimely American.

His wingspan smothering that egoistic shore
of course, all offspring departed forever,
determined to circle back to bow
before abominable stone rings on rusty fingers.

Now with compass and longitude
mead and wine to foggy hand
we meet him as we are leaving anywhere,
knowing an iceberg never meets the equator.

Ann Walsh
Yea, and Verily

IN THE FIRST YEAR the Prophet came to the mountain and the disciples gathered in the shade of his beard to hear his words.

AND the Prophet spake thus, 'So ye believe that ye can be writers? Well, then, best get on with it.'

AND I heard the Prophet's words and took heed and battled mightily with pen and typewriter, and the sweat did bead my brow and yea, verily, the very bones of my body were tormented by the outpourings of my soul.

AND the Prophet looked on my words with kindness, and guided my hand, and shared with me many libations and moments of laughter.

AND it came to pass that the time was fulfilled that the Prophet should leave the mountain.

AND the disciples were sore distressed, the publican also, and the throngs departed, each to a place where the blackflies were less multitudinous.

AND I pondered the Prophet's words and did persevere, and diligently set on paper the movings of my mind, labouring for many months and remembering always his counsel.

AND in the second year the Prophet returned to the mountain, and with great fear in my heart I did beseech him, 'Oh, mentor, take this that I have written, and guide me through the valley of revision.'

AND the Prophet looked on my words and was pleased and said unto me, 'Send thou this manuscript out into the world that it may search for a publisher.'

AND verily, I did as he bade, and the manuscript flew speedily from my hands and returned forthwith. And with great sorrowing and rending of my clothes I did again send my many pages out into the world, and again and again did they return to me until I was filled with much sadness and a sore distemper afflicted all my household.

AND in the third year the Prophet returned to the mountain, and I knelt at his feet bearing libations and cried, 'Oh, learned one, a great publisher has looked with favour on my manuscript and IT SHALL BE PUBLISHED, yea and verily!'

AND the Prophet smiled and spake thus, 'Thou hast gotten on with it, luv.'

Charles Lillard
Wells

Creature comfortable –
A hound dozed in the middle of this dusty road
All afternoon in that strong heat,
And the only movement outside our window
Was that dog scratching, now
And again all afternoon.

2

That wayaway day retains a startling clarity.
It's my earliest memory of this place, mid-July 1962.
Now all that highnoon light is bruised with darkness,
Sullen tourists follow their children to and fro –
And there's worse to come.
The voices are gone, Robin. The voices have fled.

3

We both know what I'm talking about; not voices
Per se, anyone able to separate symbol from meaning,
Or shadows from the damp, hears the resonance
Of Gold in Cariboo! It's the passion for bedrock
Speaking in the crannies and hollows, fingertips
Considering stone, its colour and symmetry;
Hardfought lives used to such unlimited freedom,
Death altered its shape not theirs.
Those voices – that's what I came seeking;
Whispers along the periphery,
The difference between pyrites and gold.

4

After this town's buttoned down,
When frost is hard in the ground
And snow's closed the passes,
Winter, circa 1860
You're the last man in the from the creeks –
The sprung horizons
Of stone, of stone full of the wind's flight
Glistening like northwater in your wary eyes.
That's how I see you, dry and irascible until
Later, yesterday already forgotten,
Tomorrow unwinding.
And I believe this sight:
You're as much miner as artist,
You've touched nothing lightly.

5

THE BALLAD OF BILLY BARKER, *Recurrence*
And the many others – the atmospherics,
Yes, THEY CALL IT THE CARIBOO tracked the image
Back to its source, but you came too late
As I understand time today
To find gold in the grass roots, or
Nuggets to be had for the washing.
Yet you've gone down to hardpan again
And repeatedly, where the oldest streams flowed,
Nourished by your own prospecting,
The difference between pyrites and gold.

6

But what of the voices?
You were here weeks ago; did they follow you
Home through the hills, believing you'd struck
The mother lode this time; their constant
Obsession, yours too,
The pure ore heart-deep in this country.

Eugene Benson
Robin the Chairman

THOUGHTS OF ROBIN SKELTON almost immediately evoke in his friends images of him in one of his roles as poet or editor or professor or anthologist or occultist ... but rarely of him as a man of affairs, as doer, as Chairman. Probably that is because we have been led to think of the artist as a being wedded to solitude and contemplation ('Like a poet hidden / In the light of thought'). But that is a Shelleyan idea contradicted by the lives of such writers as Chaucer (a diplomat), Shakespeare (a theatre manager) and, in our own time, Wallace Stevens (an insurance executive). Certainly Robin Skelton has published some 60 books covering half a dozen genres, but we should also remember that he was the man who founded the Department of Creative Writing at the University of Victoria and chaired it in its first crucial years. And anyone who still retains some notion of universities as ivory towers remote from intrigue and power play knows little about Canadian institutions of higher learning.

Robin Skelton's election as the tenth chairman of the Writers' Union of Canada was interesting for a number of reasons. He was best known as a poet and none of the nine past chairmen – Engel, Gibson, Stein, Findley, Taylor, Schroeder, Callwood, Horwood, Atwood – had been (primarily) poets. Robin was also the first full-time academic to become chairman – writers, with some cause, I believe, are wary of getting too close to the groves of Academe. Finally, Robin proved (as did Andreas Schroeder) that one didn't have to be one of the Toronto Literary Mafia to be chairman; he held down his teaching job while commuting monthly to Toronto to conduct the Union's business.

I hadn't known Robin Skelton well before I became his vice-chairman for the 1982-1983 term, although I knew his work quite well. In 1979 when Macmillan of Canada commissioned me to write a book on the Irish dramatist J.M. Synge, I read all the relevant critical studies, including Robin's three books on Synge. His work was easily the best, combining scholarship with a fellow artist's appreciation for Synge's mastery of language and dramatic technique. During 1982-1983 I came to know Robin better and as I remember him one quality stands out above all others – the sense of presence he conveyed. Some artists have been unlucky in their looks and physical presence – Oliver Goldsmith and Toulouse-Lâutrec, for example. Others, like Tennyson and Brahms (and

Robin) have looked like what their admirers imagined artists should look like. Robin is a large, powerful man and he has a fine face and profile. Most striking are his hands and his rings. He wears eight rings chosen with care from his collection, a collection which is ever growing since his friends and admirers send them to him (as they do walking sticks) from across Canada and around the world. As he talks, smokes, drinks, laughs, gesticulates, the hands are constantly in motion, the rings hypnotizing, persuading, dazzling, pointing to solutions or areas of reconciliation.

The National Council of the Writers' Union always meets twice a year for two days at 24 Ryerson Avenue just off Queen Street West in Toronto and I remember vividly Robin leading us, hour after hour, through our agenda. At our first meeting in the fall of 1982 I was puzzled by his chairmanship. It seemed too leisurely, too tolerant of council members and their foibles. I'd seen the Horwood / Callwood / Atwood trio at work and immediately admired their no-nonsense, incisive, quite *obviously* brilliant style. And yet at the end of that fall meeting when we adjourned, early, for lunch, I was surprised to note that we had covered the agenda in remarkable detail. On another occasion, at the 1983 Annual General Meeting, I saw Robin in the kind of difficulty that a Charles Taylor would have handled quite easily, the difficulty arising from a difficult motion that had received too many amendments. Robin (literally) threw up his hands, declaring that he was lost, and called on Mary Jacquest, the Union's Administrative Director, for help. The membership, seeing he was in trouble, immediately simplified the resolution and passed it without debate – or amendments. A ploy on the chairman's part?

I got to know Robin very well that year since we talked often on the telephone, met as often as possible, and conducted an intermittent correspondence. Our letters usually concerned Union business but there was room for intellectual horseplay. Reads one such letter to me:

Nothing much else to report. I've been scribbling hard, have finished the first draft of a novel, completed a few short stories, and perpetrated (as a kind of holiday task) quantities of light verse – clerihews, double dactyls, nonsense verse, and so forth. This one may cause you to groan: –

W.B. Yeats
when asked about the rates

for Thoor Ballylee
said 'This inn is free.'

Not to be outdone I replied with my own verse:

Erwin Piscator
Was not piscatorial
But he *was*
Directorial.

The National Council used to stay at the Victoria Hotel, 56 Yonge Street. It was Toronto's best buy in accommodation in 1982-1983 – about $20.00 for a spartan room that had no bath, telephone or TV. The hotel looked seedy, conveying a sense of cheap sex and ambiguous life styles. But the bar, an ornate Edwardian bar, is a glorious place and there, after our day's business was completed, the Council used to adjourn for drinks – Wright and Robinson of British Columbia, Merna Summers of Alberta, Edna Elford, the Prairie / NWT representative, Erna Paris and Jack MacLeod of Ontario, Bruce Armstrong of the Atlantic provinces, while Robin presided over our talk with geniality and with a capacity (like Socrates') to drink any of us under the table. And as the Irish whisky flowed (Robin would drink no other), we talked of everyday things – family, friends, politics, others' indiscretions, money. We also talked business – the sudden growth in the number of literary agents in Canada and the need to have some sort of writer-literary agent code; the need to push the sale of the Limited Special Edition of books by Robert Kroetsch, Jack Hodgins and Margaret Atwood to raise funds for the Union; whether we should buy a microcomputer for the office. But Robin talked most about his dream of having the Writers' Union open not just to prose writers but to poets. These and many other things we talked of in the bar of the Victoria Hotel that year and many of them came to pass.

Yes, Robin Skelton's year as Chairman of the Writers' Union of Canada was a very good year.

June Callwood
A Bit Tetched

Robin Skelton is
   smart, funny, wise
  responsible

    honourable
     kind

 a bit tetched

   and a friend.

Love,

June Callwood

Joe Rosenblatt

A Sonnet Honouring Robin Skelton
and His Muse on His Sixtieth Birthday

In a fishbowl a miniature umbrella folds
at an hour when moths and flying mice
trouble the brittle bones of hallucination:
every solarium conceals a slumber room
where pilgrims are ushered in by a spotted ghost
who oscillates a welcome upon their visitation;
'the evening's young,' he gloats, 'let's conjoin
with others on my carpet of agglutinated pleasure.'

The golden fools agree and flick their awkward fins.
Secure as spawn fermenting 'neath some protective pebbles,
happily they throb past the keeper of an alabescent gate
and jive between those petals into a deep hydraulic mind.
Frolicking where it'll never rain, bleed, or shine
I scatter these sonorities upon a granite bed.

Florence Vale
With Tongue in Cheek

In a hat to protect her from bees
Nana melted away Zuk's deep freeze
    And remarked that his rod
    Looked attractively mod
As she squeezed it between vinyl knees.

'The French Girl', pen and ink by Florence Vale.

Diane Keating
In Search of Zuk

The following taped interview with Nana, Zuk's official mistress, is printed by the kind permission of the *Modern Erotica Quarterly,* Volume xx.

As if from a woodcut, Nana's cottage squats on the rim of the forest. In the silence that eases a hot summer day into dusk, I push through a lawless garden of rose vines. There are curtains in the window and smoke curling out of the chimney. Without warning the door opens and I am led into a egg-shaped windowless den.

Nine bird cages, intricately made of rib and finger bones, hang from the ceiling. Inside each is a parrot with a brilliant beak. They begin a litany of 'Inward, Inward to the Sacred Cave'. The walls are adorned with the stuffed and glass-eyed heads of men, but what dominates is a magnificent black high-heeled boot, spotlit, on a mirrored pedestal.

At the other end of the room, buttocks – all of them extra large and male – are cushions arranged in a half circle beside a stone fireplace. When I sit down a fire flares in the grate. The whips on the mantle slither off, disappearing between the floor boards. I take out my tape recorder and test it by uttering a Zukism. 'The error of novelty is the belief that it is new, rather than another expression of the search after essence ...'

NANA enters. She is elegant and severe in her silver vinyl pant suit. The geometry of her face and its reflections are cold, almost metallic. Given her shaved head and long bare feet, I think of the moon ... Nana ... mirror of the night.

A shadow dances around her. 'This is Phzeff,' she says. It slips through me like a sea breeze. During our conversation which lasts three hours, NANA moves about the room as if on ice melting into water.

NANA: When I first met Zuk, he stood behind me in a queue waiting for a footpath across the void. As the sun rose, so did the warmth between my legs, bathing my maidenhead in dawn. Sex was an egg cracking with yellow light. Looking down, I found the cause of my first sexual revelation was a small mirror in the shape of an eye attached to an ivory cane. The sun caromed off the mirror and sent a shaft of light under my skirt, along my thigh.

Leaning on the cane was a transparent plastic raincoat. It

contained a naked man who whispered: 'What has the substance of the moon and the essence of the sun?' I knew. An egg. *Between these two words* NANA *seems to slip through seven dreams.* Then he doffed his bowler hat, bowed and announced: 'I am your lost skin of light. I am the voyeur of your jade room. I am Zuk.'

INTERVIEWER: Is it true that Zuk practises the ancient art of Zen Taoism and that his guru, Bloc, is a reincarnation of Hung Ti, the yellow emperor from the Hsia Dynasty who became immortal after having sexual intercourse with 1200 women?

NANA: Zuk never discussed belief. He once said: 'The discussion of beliefs is the world of Woody Allen.' Myself, I distrust abstraction as a shadow distrust a veil. *Phzeff throws handfuls of sparks that look like laughter, except in the darkening corners where they turn into anger.*

INTERVIEWER: Most scholars agree that you are the axle of Zuk's original doctrine of sexual ecstasy. You are also a descendent of de Sade, and by the age of twenty had won the Ramhorn Prize for your re-enactment as digital art of his *One Hundred and Twenty Days in Sodom.* Have these facts any bearing on each other?

NANA: Does the hole pertain to the whole? Zuk discovered the hidden entrance in the shift of cranial plates in a woman's skull and could, therefore, change an orgasm into a miracle.

After hours of mouthing each toe, each finger, they uncurled into fern fronds. My nipples bloomed into lilies ... symbolic of the Immaculate Conception. While blood thundered, Zuk's cock was transformed into a lightning bolt that plunged the cold opening to my brain. Rain, falling copiously from heaven, sprouted the noumena; but Zuk, a sexual mystic, knew how to escape flooding emotion and quicksand around the soul.

It was the ultimate wet dream, NANA *laughs stormily* cerebral copulation stropped on the philosopher's stone.

INTERVIEWER: There's an academic controversy, led by Dr. Krok, concerning the perversions of Zuk's eroticism. Could you tell us why the mechanics of de Sade were significant to your relationship?

NANA: But they were not. The wheels and pulleys of de Sade's sexuality are only the engineering of his eighteenth-century soul. His exhilaration at the angle of penetration, his enthusiasm for the devexity of the whip are monkish habits acquired in the cells of rehabilitation. De Sade was, at heart, a Rotarian: a man searching for the common denominator in cruelty. There was nothing common about Zuk. NANA *exhales light, scaring Phzeff who is curled on her lap.*

INTERVIEWER: In your collection of poetry, *Fleshsongs and Supplications,* you refer to the shape shifting of Zuk's brain. Could you be more explicit?

NANA: His brain, born in the image of a hungry she-wolf, terrified his teachers who sheared it – hoping for a lamb – but they got a werewolf ... a demented voluptuous creature that Zuk kept caged in pataphysics and zen-surrealism. However, when he was fucking, the beast's craving took over. A shock to unsuspecting lovers, especially soft idolatrous students unaware of the hunger in his head.

Like lovers in French novels, Zuk and I met at tea-time ... that slender space between day and night. Naked, except for thigh boots and a long slippery whip, I arched before him like a cat that loves no one. His frenzied brain would escape, but with strokes of hot wet silk I subdued it, and we would have an orgasm so powerful that yin and yang fused ... pushing us into a re-birth.

INTERVIEWER: Then you, in your role as Zuk's mistress, were also like every artist, attempting a more absolute and complete reality. One that transcends the moment, 'la petite mort'. Did Zuk have other idiosyncracies and did they affect his style of love making?

NANA: Zuk's style was the sound of one hand closing which eventually led to his interest in cults of invisibility. As for other idiosyncracies, I suppose his Burmese bell would do. It's a hand-made device, slightly smaller than a wild plum, which is implanted at the source point of a woman's orgasm.

When it came to locating that whirlpool of my soul, Zuk's cock was a divining rod. The foot is the map of the body so he began by licking the soles of my feet. At a point on my instep, a tidal wave began along the fourth rib on my sinister side. I imagined rainbow trout copulating in golden coves. As his tongue – the gift of the unspoken word – lapped my flesh, the source point of joy intensified its luminous flux. Zuk became every man I ever loved ... the pungent odours ... the briny taste of our origins in the sea.

The fiery storm never ended until, placing his mouth over my wound of heaven, he sucked out my soul ... my body imploding into a black hole dense with its own dross.

After placing the soul inside a Burmese bell Zuk gently eased it back to mark, like a buoy, the vortex of my rapture. 'A poem for the Big Bang,' he told me. A birth by fire that left a cloud of ash on his breath and my sex drowning.

Once embedded, the bell's ceaseless rustle – like wings of a hippogriff crossing the swollen moon – kept me in constant yearning. Everything touched me as if I lived at the base of stars.

My eyes glimmered, Zuk noted in his journal, 'like votive candles in a Catholic church.'

INTERVIEWER: What about Adrienne whom Zuk named Dauntless Eve. Is her vagina a flame-throwing poppy, a buttercup trickling creaminess or a mocking canterbury bell?

NANA: *with a dark smile, eyebrows lifting like dragonfly wings* Ahh you know from studying Zuk that true lust depends upon our glorious ability to imagine. He once told me that to think of Adrienne was to crouch over burning coals in a snow storm. Her sex was a tigerlily radiating paradox. She posed for Zuk with thighs spread like splashes of moonlight over the face of her quadriplegic lover. While his tongue – with the throbbing delicacy of a ruby hummingbird – darted in and out of her swollen bud, she dreamed of riding naked on a manticore through Times Square.

INTERVIEWER: What about the Marvellous Eye? We are told that it's an Optician's shop sign, but later we are told that Adrienne's his chosen mistress. Does this occur because, to quote Zuk, 'everything is everything else, especially after the act of love'?

NANA: The Marvellous Eye, as perceiver of the inner Cosmos, is an erotic symbol. Every thirty-three years a jet-black goat with white horns and hooves appears on a Himalayan mountain peak. In a ceremony originated by a twelfth-century Tibetan Lama, this demi-divine beast is sacrificed and its eyelids with long, silky lashes removed, buried in quick-lime then steamed in a bamboo basket. The process is repeated seven times to ensure its all-seeing powers.

INTERVIEWER: You are arranging for the Satyr Gallery in New York to hold an exhibition of Zuk's drawings. Can you describe them? Do they embody the same self-adjusting sensuality as his writing?

NANA: The drawings represent Zuk's most intense reality. He believed that the vagina was a face without eyes ... the face of a flower ... and if anyone took the time to understand its being they would know supreme enlightenment. His last years were devoted to the cult of the cunt.

Zuk sketched these secret flowers during the flesh-coloured glow of a spring dawn when shadows danced like cupids and bodies blossomed into apple trees. He knew that drawing, like making love, is a breaking apart. I overheard him say to Bloc that, if he were God, he would take every cunt and gently place it among the most brilliant wild flowers in the meadow. Instead, when each lay open and glistening from his touch, he took a Japanese brush and, with colour mixed from earth and heart blood, planted it on paper.

It's impossible to describe the incandescence of his drawings. If Henry Miller and Georgia O'Keefe had fucked they might have brought to one such profound voluptuousness of seeing ... such unlimited potentiality for expansion. My favourite drawing? The old-fashioned white rose of the Countess who opened her seamless purple robe and kneeled in the convent of the Immaculate Heart of Mary. As Zuk sketched she stroked her bulging petals with one long red nail ... collecting the drops of milky dew in a green glass bottle.

By a kink in Zuk's fate, the goat's eyelid was in the pocket of a raincoat which the Widow bought for him at a garage sale. While fucking he would slip it over the end of his penis, transforming it into a Third Eye ... a tickling eye of Zeus that sparked passion ... illuminating the endless expanse between heart beat and breath. 'Women,' Zuk told a reporter from the *Globe and Mail,* 'have the night sky within them. They obey the movement of stars. Through the moon filter of their memory they know themselves as mysteries being formed.'

INTERVIEWER: According to the RCMP files, Zuk was last seen at 7 PM, May 7th, 1977, walking toward your apartment on Rue des Anges. *A long pause. Phzeff nervously crawls into my eyes. As the room dissolves into darkness I hear Nana's voice like an echo from a mountain peak.*

NANA: Yes ... Ascension Day ... Zuk arrived, as always, at that rosebud moment when light and dark are evenly balanced. 'Teatime,' he said, as always, when I opened the door. We took off our clothes. We put out the clock. Since loving is an act of sacred cannibalism, to consume Zuk's penis – the terrestrial host – was to appropriate life. By the divine energy of semen I continuously sucked in the river of his blood ... the meadow of his skin ... the mist of his dreams ... until he disappeared into the primordial matrix of my body. Now we are one. The universe of universes.

Virgil Burnett
The Hour of the Asp

HE LIFTED HIS EYES from the page, cocked his head, and listened. There had been a sound, he thought, behind him in the empty house: a floor board creaking, or a bed frame. It was an old house, full of memorious sounds.

Whatever it was, it was not repeated. He shrugged, looked about the study at the book-lined walls, at the heaped papers, at the other chair – the green chair, as he still thought of it, although years of fading had left its shabby velvet essentially colourless. He also still thought of it as her chair.

He rubbed his eyes, then went back to the poem he was reading. It was a long poem, wise and funny, quite brilliant in its way, he thought, not that many would notice, or care if they did. He was very near the end of it. The notion of being finished, of having no more lines to play with, to muse over, made him melancholy.

'How gentle,' he read aloud, 'is the kiss....'

Again he broke off. Now it seemed to him that there was something in the garden. He laid aside his book and rose to his feet.

'I'm going to have a look around,' he said, as if to someone who might be sitting in the faded velvet chair.

Standing under the evergreens behind the house, he strained to hear, to see. There was nothing. The breeze of the afternoon had died entirely away. It was too late in the season for insect activity and the few remaining birds had gone to roost. There used to be a barn owl living in the old coach house attic but not in several years had he heard its eery shuddering cry. Sometimes cats or dogs or raccoons poked about. Tonight there was nothing. Even the lake, which could usually be heard grumbling at the dunes, was silent.

'How gentle is the kiss ...,' he murmured again, perhaps only to challenge the quiet.

As if in reply a pine-cone detached itself from a twig and tumbled earthward, bouncing leisurely from branch to branch on its descent of eighty, ninety feet to the ground. The noise it made falling, though modest enough, was exaggerated to loudness by the night's abnormal silence.

He shivered. Already the air had more winter in it than summer. Raw as it was, he resisted going back into the house, almost as if he were expecting something to happen in the garden, or hoping something might.

'A coronary,' he suggested to the void, like a man asking to have a prescription filled, 'a massive one, if you please.'

When finally he did go inside, he was not only cold and gloomy but restless as well. Instead of returning to the study, he wandered vaguely here and there, opening and shutting doors, rummaging about the dim passages and vacant rooms of the house.

Timidly, like a tourist in a Stately Home, he made a circuit of the dining-room, moving slowly up one side of the refectory table, then down the other. Each of the twelve high-backed chairs, so austere in their emptiness, seemed to mock him as he passed. From the fireplace, which was as black and cheerless behind its screen as a Victorian graveyard crypt, came a stench of cold ash. At the end of the table closest to the kitchen he put out his hand and touched the smooth maple. His fingers left a mark in the dust, a meaningless calligramme.

He stood for a while at the doorway to the parlour but did not enter. The room seemed too large for him to try to occupy alone. Besides, he did not like the rug; he never had. Like many carpets, it had a floral pattern, which was nothing in itself – certainly he did not object to flowers – but this design reminded him of waterlilies, and waterlilies reminded him, at certain times anyway, of a pond he had known as a child, a stagnant pool where once he had seen a drowned kitten floating among black leathery pads and waxen nenuphars.

Tonight of course was one of those times. Even from the doorway he fancied that he could see the cat – there beneath the coffee table or yonder by the chaise longue – a pathetic little cadaver, sodden and bloated, with a cord about its neck.

The unused bedrooms smelled of mildew. He did not mind it but opened several windows nevertheless, wondering as he did what it was that made him suppose mildew to have a female fragrance.

In the kitchen he poured himself a drink – rye, rather a lot of it, in a sherry glass. He had meant to take it with him back to the study, had meant to sip it while he read, but as soon as it was poured, he drank it off directly in gulps instead of sips.

The closets were the worst of all, especially the one in the hall by the front door with its accumulation, two decades old, of raincoats and boots and other wet day paraphernalia. It broke his heart. The slick surfaces, the aggressive odour of rubberized fabric and fishy plastic made him so sick with longing that his guts griped and his gonads ached.

Without any purpose he began to take down the coats, looking carefully at each, trying to remember their provenances. With boots and hats he did the same. Indifferent to taboos he opened all the umbrellas. He handled all the walking sticks, most of which he had cut himself for this one or that one. Abandoned here in the dark closet, they seemed infinitely forlorn.

When he left the hall, the floor behind him was everywhere strewn with foul weather togs and gear, almost as if a band of children had been playing at charades or circus or some other dress-up game.

At last he returned to the study. For a longer time than he knew, he sat motionless in his chair looking out upon the night, but eventually he took up his book and ruffled through its pages until he found his place.

'I've almost finished my book,' he said to the woman who was no longer there.

And when I am finished, he asked himself, what shall I do? Shall I read it again? Backward perhaps, or upside down? Maybe I should try it wearing a blindfold or one of those black hoods that hangmen provide for their clients.

Behind him in the empty house a floor board creaked, or a bed frame. Now he paid no attention, but cleared his throat and began to read, mumbling the words just barely aloud, without expression, without feeling, but doggedly, like a weary monk bent on the fulfilment of his compline obligation.

How gentle is the kiss
of the asp on the nipple,
how brutal the lunge
of the nipple at the asp....

(Hommage à Georges Zuk)

Ludwig Zeller
As to How Georges Zuk Asks Robin Skelton, His Double, to Turn Stones into Whisky by Means of Magic *

Much waiting makes me grow ten fangs
Dear friend, listen to me: we all carry
Inside us a skeleton that burns with thirst
Becomes a beast and lurks;
In each one of us the wolf descends to drink from the well
Feathers and scales become smoke.

One must wear glasses against dizziness,
Fill the pitcher with terrifying stones
And, if possible, tie to one's back a barrel
Its ribs split-open, shriek like women
Screaming. You make them spin, push
With their breasts burning the wood with laughter.

Venus, close your eyes, mix the black pebbles
With the blue, the green with the yellow. Make the poet
Whisper enchantments on the edge of the glass:
Three little grains of salt can sometimes
Give liquor the taste of tears.
Take the beam out of your eye and then repeat
Three times: Zuk, Zik, Zek! Now backwards. You've got it!

The years don't make us older, it is life we celebrate.
When raising the glass one plumbs the must,
Dancing on a wire, madly turning, like utter fools,
One doesn't kiss, rather, bites the forbidden fruit.

Cheers, Robin Skelton!
When we get to be a hundred, tell silky
Venus to repeat the miracle in your verse.

*English version by Beatriz Zeller

De como Georges Zuk Pide a su Doble Robin Skelton, que por Efectos de la Magia, Haga con Piedras Whisky.

Me crecen de esperar los diez colmillos,
Querido amigo, escucha: todos llevamos
Dentro un esqueleto que arde en la sed
Y convertido en bestia nos acecha;
En cada uno el lobo baja a beber al pozo
Y las plumas y escamas se hacen humo.

Hay que ponerse gafas para el vértigo,
Llenar con piedras de terror el cántaro
Y si es posible, atarse a las espaldas un tonel
Cuyas costillas se abran, chillen como mujeres
Dando gritos. Se las hace dar vueltas, empujar
Con los pechos hasta quemar de risa las maderas.

Cierra tus ojos Venus, mezcla guijarros negros
Con azules, verdes con amarillos. Haz que el poeta
Susurre encantamientos en el borde del vaso:
Tres granitos de sal pueden a veces,
Dar al licor el gusto de las lágrimas.
Saca entonces del ojo la gran viga, repitiendo
Tres veces ¡Zuk, Zik, Zek! Al revés, y ¡lo has logrado!

Los años no se cumplen, se celebra la vida
Cuando al alzar la copa se penetra en el mosto,
Se baila en un alambre, se gira loco, loco de remate
No se besa, se muerde la fruta prohibida.

        ¡Salud, Robin Skelton!
Cuando cumplamos cien, haz que Venus
Sedosa, repita por tus versos el milagro.

'The Magician', collage 1978 by Ludwig Zeller.

Brian Wilson
Skelton and Magic: An Interview

BRIAN WILSON: One aspect of your life that no one ever seems to say much about is your interest in magic. You've written two books on the subject (*Spellcraft* and *Talismanic Magic*), and I suspect that the whole business is pretty important to you. How did it all start?

ROBIN SKELTON: During my teens and early twenties I experienced several trance-like dreams of a woman figure whom Robert Graves would certainly have identified as the Goddess, but it wasn't until my early thirties that I began to make spells.

I had been reading Alexander Carmichael's *Carmina Gadelica*, a compendium of Gaelic folk poems, most of which are spells and charms. A small child, the daughter of a friend, had a serious fall and was unconscious. It looked as if she must have broken quite a number of bones. I said to myself, 'Well, you're supposed to be a poet, and you've been reading all these spells, so why not make one.' I made one, and the child woke up with only a few bruises.

I dismissed this as coincidence, of course, but then another similar crisis occurred, and then others, and when I found my healing spells were achieving about eighty per cent success, I began to take the whole thing more seriously, and to study all I could find about witchcraft.

BRIAN WILSON: The word 'witchcraft' gets bandied about a lot, though. I can't really picture you holding Black Sabbaths and conjuring up the devil. What exactly do you mean by that? Can you define it?

ROBIN SKELTON: Witchcraft, or Wicca, or the Craft, as it's often called, has nothing to do with the devil. It originated in a pre-Christian folk religion which celebrates the changing seasons of the year, and personifies the life-force as a Goddess and Her consort. It holds that you can use your own psychic power – or you could call it energy field – to improve the quality of life. The witches' law is: 'Do what you will, and harm no one.' Also, 'Perfect love, perfect trust.'

Some witches work in groups, or covens. I usually work alone, except when I have a really difficult job that needs more than one person's energy; then I get other witches to join with me. When I was initiated as a Witch I was named as a 'Spellcaster', and that's what I do. I cast mostly healing spells. Certainly no curses. And I make talismans. My most successful one so far is to cure insomnia.

But while I recognize that ceremonials and rituals are necessary when you work in a group, simply to get everyone of the same mind, I distrust the over-elaborate ritual. It can simply become theatre. And the leader of elaborate ceremonies and rituals may become an authoritarian figure – which I dislike. I see the Craft as fundamentally democratic, even anarchic in its having no highly formalized social structure.

BRIAN WILSON: I guess most of the spells you're describing have to do with your private life. Does witchcraft come into your poetry at all? Does it provide you with a Muse figure, like the White Goddess does for Robert Graves?

ROBIN SKELTON: The Muse crops up fairly frequently in my work from the late fifties onward, but not as a definite Goddess of the Witches. I mean, I don't give her labels. She's simply there, in Her various guises as the Maiden, the Mother, and the Crone who is the layer-out of the dead. She is the woman who crops up in a lot of my love poems – which are not, as some have supposed, strictly autobiographical. If I'd had as many love affairs as that, I'd never have had time to write the poems! I suppose my most extreme expression of the Muse-poet relationship is in my 'Nine Poems for the Muse', of 1970, but She is also the centre of my long poem, 'The Dark Window', which was published in 1962.

BRIAN WILSON: You've written quite a lot about the stylistics of ancient witchcraft – for example, you deal with the incantatory poem or chant at length in *Spellcraft*. Do you use that form consciously in your own work? Or modify it in some way?

ROBIN SKELTON: Some love poems are certainly bidding spells, attempting to bring the desired person to the side – or the bed – of the speaker. But I see poems as being essentially dramatic monologues, not confessions. In most cases the lover is a projection of part of myself, a sort of role I'm playing – though I'm playing it seriously, exploring the man-woman relationship. Yes, a good many are incantatory, but my real incantations I do not publish. These are private matters, calling up the Muse to give me the power to make poems or, of course, do magical work. I've published one or two true spells, but mostly spells make bad poetry. In a spell you have to be authoritative, assured, definite – you mustn't speculate or qualify or hesitate. And poems that don't speculate, or doubt, or possess ambiguities are often a bit boring. Though there are, of course, splendid exceptions.

BRIAN WILSON: It's well established that repetitive chanting can have a powerful effect on a group of people. Do you consciously manipulate language to achieve a special magical effect?

ROBIN SKELTON: With very few exceptions, my poems are intended to be spoken aloud, and I do pay a lot of attention to the sound they make, to assonance and consonance, to the rise and fall of the voice and the changes in speed. I've learned a few tricks from the Welsh system of harmony, cynghanedd. Whether that's magical in any real sense I don't know, but certainly, if a poem is effective it does affect the thought and emotions of the hearer. So perhaps that is a sort of magic. Certainly when I perform my poems I'm aware of using the same kind of psychic energy that I use when I'm making a magical incantation. But I feel it too when I'm lecturing and get 'turned on' by my subject. So maybe it's a matter of 'projecting' as an actor 'projects' on stage.

BRIAN WILSON: Nobody could fail to notice that you wear a different ring on each finger. And right now you're wearing a pentagram pendant. Where does this all fit in with your vision of witchcraft?

ROBIN SKELTON: For some reason most witches I know are a bit addicted to jewellery. I think it's partly because well-chosen rings, bracelets and pendants are felt to be talismanic, to contain energy and to transmit it to the wearer, rather like small radios. Some of my rings appeal to me because they are symbolic of something or other, often in a purely private fashion. Others have sentimental associations. Still others I simply thought were beautiful. I wear a pentagram pendant because the pentagram symbolizes the unity of flesh and spirit, of yin and yang, of the five senses – and a good deal more. It is one of the oldest symbols we know and predates Judaism by thousand of years, though it is, together with the hexagram, connected in the legend of King Solomon. There's a vast lore to do with precious and semi-precious stones, of course, but honestly, I don't pay too much attention to it myself, though I wrote about it in *Talismanic Magic*.

BRIAN WILSON: All right, we know a little bit now about the interplay between witchcraft and your poetry. But apart from that, do you practise it on a day-to-day basis?

ROBIN SKELTON: It isn't a daily activity. I mean, I don't cast a spell a day or anything like that. But I do make magic fairly frequently. It is almost invariably healing magic, and I can only do that for people I have actually met. I'm limited in that respect. I have to have sensed their personalities, as it were. So, over the last ten years when I've been growing more and more involved with the Craft, I've tackled a good many disorders, including warts, sprains, stomach upsets, glaucoma, kidney stones, mild arthritis, earache, migraine – quite a variety now I come to think of it. But I never do anything unless I have a doctor's diagnosis as a guide.

I've learned also to use what might be called the 'laying on of hands', which is interesting. I don't always actually touch the person, but I send energy out from the palm of my hand, and it is usually felt as a minor electric shock or a mild heat.

I lift curses, too. That's sometimes a bit tricky as you have to track down the origin of the curse. One woman was in a dreadful state and I tracked the trouble down to a ring she had been given by her dead husband, who had made it into a malign talisman – probably unintentionally. The woman was near to having a nervous breakdown, and at first blush you'd have thought she was paranoid. Well, I took the ring, which she wore all the time, away from her, cleansed it, and gave it her back. She's fine now. I tried a talisman to get one character employment. He got the kind job he wanted within four or five weeks.

Some of this may well be auto-suggestion, of course – the placebo principle – but what the hell! I don't care if it's entirely psychological or magical at all as long as it helps. Some witches use legerdemain to reinforce the faith of the patient and are dismissed as charlatans; that seems a bit superficial to me. If I convince you that you will get well by sucking at the sore place and then spitting out fake blood, the conviction may be all you need. There is psychosomatic healing as well as psychosomatic sickness, after all.

I sometimes 'cleanse' houses of what used to be called 'bad vibes' and I've helped another witch in exorcism, though I've not yet done a full-dress exorcism myself. Oh, there are lots of things I find myself doing, but I'm very careful. One must not meddle too much with people's lives. I won't cast love spells for people – but I will tell them how to do it themselves.

Of course, I celebrate the changes of the seasons with rituals at the appropriate times, the Witches' sabbats. My rituals are very short and simple. I don't think one can keep up the concentration for long periods, myself. I do these with my family, and sometimes other people join in. I could go on for ever about this. It is, after all, important to me. And I get very cross with these sensationalist books about the Craft that portray witches as spending their time cooking up curses and sex spells and so forth.

Many witches do more than I. A good many are expert herbalists, which I am not, and though I do occasionally use numerology and runes, I don't use the Tarot, and I'm hopeless at astrology. So I'm very limited, really. I basically just cast spells in the service of my religion, which is emphatically a religion of love and, I should add, opposed to no other religion. Witches don't seek converts; it's against their principles. And witches do not regard other religions as evil. There is truth in every religion, though religious organizations sometimes appear to be doing their best to distort it. But I am rambling ...

BRIAN WILSON: Have you joined any group or coven?

ROBIN SKELTON: No. I sometimes get together with one or more of my witch friends and we talk things over, or maybe do some work together if it's necessary, as I've said, and that's all.

BRIAN WILSON: You explained in *Spellcraft* that it takes a great deal of energy to make a spell, and your writing must also demand very intense energy. How do you manage both writing and witchcraft?

ROBIN SKELTON: I remember Thomas Kinsella saying to me, years ago in Dublin, 'God is good, fits back to burden.' I guess I just go on doing what I have to do, and the energy is provided most of the time. Sometimes, yes, after a difficult spell I am exhausted for twenty-four hours and can't write. Sometimes after I've been writing I have no energy for magic – though it is easier to summon up the energy for magic than the 'inspiration' for a poem. Still, in magic as in poetry, I get 'dry patches' when I can't really manage anything, which is very upsetting when there's work to be done.

BRIAN WILSON: Can you sum it all up for us in terms of results? Have you and your work derived lasting benefits from your exploration of witchcraft?

ROBIN SKELTON: That's a difficult one. How can I tell if my work would have been better or worse if I'd had another set of beliefs. I do feel certain, though, that the Craft has given me strength and a balanced view of life. It has often made me feel useful, because I can help people and don't have to wring my hands in total helplessness when a friend is ill. Even if my spells fail to work, they do prevent me feeling frustrated. And it is good to have rituals that make one feel in touch with the natural world, with the seasons, with growing things – even though, paradoxically, I'm not attracted by gardening. It has led me also to explore many fascinating aspects of mysticism, religion, social history, even some of the latest views of the quantum physicists about the nature of time, and of course all aspects of extra-sensory perception.

So I could say it has enriched my life, given me new viewpoints, provided me with fresh ways to explore, fresh speculations. It is now so much a part of life that I can't see myself without it. It is a religion, after all, and one that is based firmly upon love and life-acceptance without being shackled by rigorous moral codes and an authoritarian priesthood. I am comfortable with it. And in as much as I feel benefited by it, I must assume that my poetry has benefited too, for poetry has always been an inextricable part of my life.

Keith Maillard
Dear Robin

I BEGIN AND cast my own spell to invoke you, and I can see you now, your hands extended and moving. Sandy has a cold, her sinuses clogged, and you are casting your spell. The concentration is electric – a psychic Van de Graaff generator – and I can almost see the electricity arc from your hands to her face.

But no, damn it, that's not right. I've heard you talk about how easily mere literature intrudes. Once you showed Michael how to transmute an anecdote he'd just told you into a poem. So what *is* the process then, exactly what? No, it's not in the least like a generator, and I can see no electricity; I was making that up because it was easy. *This* is right: Sandy is fit and muscular but not a slender woman; standing before you, she appears slender. You are so much larger than she is; you are solid, substantial, bear-like. But it's not merely the contrast, it's something else, and here's where you told Michael to persist – to the image and the word, finally to all that will be left after the quiver has passed, to the text on the page. *No, it is not electrical.* That was *my* internal generator of words, the one that wants me to say these too-easy things, that it's frozen in time, a memory like a photograph, a fly in amber, but it's not like that at all (although the colour clearly *is* amber). You move; memory moves. It's opening, organic, not a crystallization but a blossom in a breeze.

More clearly now, Sandy appears before you like a figure just this moment remembered; she's a wisp of melody from an old song – Celtic certainly – 'bow down', and Pound's 'petals on a wet, black bough', and, yes, this is the way – through the rich, inexhaustible oral tradition – and yes, the gabbling generator in the brain won't work, but the ancient stock phrases will: to tell the story again as it's been told again and will be told again. She's slender as a willow wand, she's a bending willow, bowing down; it's the motion of taking the snow, slowly, accumulating it, bearing the weight, then releasing it. She is wand-slender before you, a page of wands, a maiden in a tapestry, and, Robin Skelton, you're the warlock.

I did think you were wildly flamboyant when I first met you, grandly eccentric with your tattoo and mane of hair, and rings, but later I felt how natural in yourself you were, how easy you'd made the balancing act look: showing yourself to the world as yourself. And now you're making *this* look easy, whatever on earth you're doing. Your hands move but do not touch her, and Sandy moves.

You're Celtic and steeped in it to your eyeballs, and in that realm, once and future, the story was told and will be told again, as you told it when you delivered that perfect one-liner to Paddy Moloney backstage in Vancouver after the Chieftains' concert: 'Do you remember the afternoon when Marianne Faithfull was throwing up in the castle?' The Celtic realm is a magical nation, is a woman, is sovereign, so let Sandy float in that wind, golden-haired maiden in your motion, moving. But what is the wind?

Robin, I have learned important things from you, from your complexities, your multitude of books in every genre, your refusal to divide art into compartments, your play that bubbles up from the bottom like Blake's eternal delight, your solid and painstaking and *fair* criticism, your classical belles-lettres, your stories balanced on wit like vases on needles, your bumbling Professor Skelton who translates but can never quite get the point of the obscure wizard / poet Zuk, your spells, your collages, your rambling talks about anything at all. Sitting in your living-room, I've thought that you are indeed, like the good Dr. Williams, the happy genius of your household.

To tell the tale that was told before: Sandy sways before you, her eyes shut, her hair so golden it blisters the eye. She cannot see you, but she moves to your hands. This is a profoundly romantic moment. This is magic. This is a bit silly. This is ... God knows what it is. Afterward, when we are alone, I ask her what happened. Her voice is as matter of fact as a pancake. 'My sinuses drained,' she says.

Gary Snyder wrote that there 'comes a time when the poet must choose' to 'step beyond the bound onto the way out', or 'to step deep in the stream of his people, history, tradition ... to become richly foundationed and great and sane and ordered.' More simply, it's the way out or the way home. *You* are richly foundationed and great and sane and ordered.

For all your complexities, you are also a man of utter simplicity. Once at the end of the evening when you stayed with me, you said, quietly, 'It's good to have a friend.' Yes, it is. Safe home, Robin.

Love, Keith

ooloeamolearningeetooo
writennagainoleforgotoo
oethatvsvitvwasnhardoo
pullingnnthejlinessoo
downoooroundiando
ssshapingwtheplaceso
theyaymeetethespaceso
nrntheymlesseniando
widenxtheiwayatheyoi
oarelhbtallandeageroi
orohuddledoandsquat
theyywaycthatitheyoss
spelloicnotlhowliheari
itooorsayitorevenfkluic
thinkoobutxjinvjzaaai
ffashiontheyccechoose
describingccaootrackr
oiothroughcsilencemi
inisilenceansweringthe
loudworldbackkcckcc

'The Calligraphy Lesson' by Robin Skelton. Calligraphy and
Confusion by Pamela Brooks, 1985.

Greg Gatenby
Skelton as Reader

AS OF THIS WRITING, more than 800 authors have read at Harbourfront, but none has approached Robin Skelton for sartorial outrage. From the moment he enters the room in which he is to read, the audience knows The Poet has arrived. In lesser mortals, such a studied insult to Savile Row would seem an affectation designed to deflect one's attention from a probable deficiency of talent. But since we know Robin Skelton's standing as a poet is unimpeachable (even if too few are aware of the excellence of his translations from the ancient Greek), we must attribute his vestments, in part, to his perception of himself as a member of that same Celtic priesthood to which Yeats and Joyce belonged. If his clerical collar is occasionally askew, forgive the dishevelment: for he is also a witch who practises white magic – a sometimes unruly vocation.

In Toronto, there are times when a genuine blackthorn stick is necessary to beat off muggers or publishers importuning with huge advances for your next book of poems. However, in Ireland the blackthorn conveys, rather, a certain conservative dignity, a sense that the walker is not only aware of runic tradition and lyrical history but is actually pleased to be part of the continuum. This was definitely one of the impressions which Robin Skelton left on his listeners when he read in Eire on a European tour in December 1983. Interestingly, he had read in London just prior to his Irish tour and a huge bomb had exploded then at Harrods. During his tour from Cork to Sligo, several explosions happened throughout Ireland. To this day, I don't believe Interpol has made a connection – but to those privileged to sit in the damp halls of Ireland where readings are doomed to take place, the gravelly voice, the delicately interspersed erudition, the magnificent poems all combined to explosive effect. This is not a strain of metaphor: the audiences were really left stunned, and moved by the poems he read.

It was while Robin was reading in two of Ireland's most magical counties, Mayo and Connemara, that I came to know other, endearing aspects of his character which professional contact in Toronto had camouflaged. Foremost amongst these was his generosity to younger writers, a claim bellowed by several senior writers of my acquaintance with that volume mendacity alone can spawn, but practised by few. Just as important was his desire to see Canadian writers strive for world-class excellence, not regional popularity, an exhortation evident enough in *Malahat* from its earliest issues, of course, but needed more than ever now that our critics, reviewers and editors believe reading a book from another province is an act of daring internationalism. And it was in Mayo, especially, that his outlandish finger rings, literary legerdemain, the avowal of mystical verisimilitude – and most particularly the poems, revealed to me that Robin Skelton was not only a better writer than I had previously thought, but was nothing less than Canada's literary Magus.

May he so conjure for centuries to come!

John Webb
Play These Grand Things Straight:
The Poetry of Robin Skelton

ROBIN SKELTON'S POETRY has never stayed with a single voice, or
style, or school, and his output over the last 40 years has been
massive. There are lean, sparse poems packed into the centre of the
page and rollicking, traditional ballads of the kind which have
almost disappeared entirely from the landscape of contemporary
poetry; there are rhetorically polished pentameters, rich in
assonantal and alliterative music, exercises in surrealism, Welsh
forms whose names most Welshmen cannot pronounce; there are
the translations of that riotous and fictional enemy of decency,
Georges Zuk, and – most recently – the translations of the great
Hungarian poet, George Faludy, whose real life story is far more
extraordinary than the invented one of Georges Zuk.

Robin Skelton's poetry has always celebrated *place,* and the
genius of place, in Yorkshire, Cornwall, Anglesey, Ireland, and the
west coast of Canada. Since the sheer range of his work is so wide,
it isn't easy to characterize it with reference to any single theme. At
the age of sixty, a man naturally takes stock of the past and
wonders (perhaps grimly) about the future. Yet the tricks of
memory and passing time – and the way these betray the flesh and
the spirit – have been constantly recurring preoccupations
throughout Robin Skelton's poetry. As early as 1960, at the
relatively tender age of thirty-five, he had already developed a
certain gloomy grandeur about this theme:

> Half way to God only knows,
> is it a trick like the ant's scuttle,
> this all-for-art, this home-making,
> to end on the tip, a used bottle?

At forty – not quite so tender – he mournfully confesses that:

> When young
> I could amaze myself with my own stare
> and touched discovery each time I reached
> the razor to my cheek. Now nothing's new
> but comprehension. Each road I have walked
> rewards each footfall with a vacant gaze.

Although Skelton never succumbed to the cult of jaundiced middle age and the kind of calculated scepticism associated with the Movement poets of the 1950s, he rubbed shoulders with them occasionally. He was able to combine his technical mastery of prosody with the ability to give small details and ordinary domestic surfaces a visionary gleam. There are many poems in which those surfaces are recalled and re-lived with a mixture of highly-charged nostalgia and exact realism. In 'As I Remember It', for example, the poet revisits a garden shed, and finds an old picture postcard pinned to the door. The poem gives this trivial and unremarkable object an emblematic power. The picture shows:

> ... a square with pigeons and a sky
> more blue than possible, all shine and gloss,
> and ill-shaped people promenading by;
> the front was scratched, one corner tattered; why
> the thing was pinned there heaven only knows.
> As I remember it, I pulled it down.
> It's odd how a chance memory grows and grows.
>
> The card was at the back of it. The card
> it was that set me thinking of The Shed,
> and yet I almost missed it – small and bright,
> its drawing pins rusted home into the wood.
> The other side told nothing. All it said
> was 'With Best Wishes' and the name was blurred
> beyond all understanding, while the stamp
> had gone long since. The whole thing was absurd.
> And yet ...
> I felt a private glory had occurred.

Over and over again the rites of memory confer sanctity on places and objects from the past. In 'Westfield Lane', for example:

> ... an abacus
> of worlds clicks on my natal string
> five, ten, fifteen years back
> till Westfield Lane, a scoop and climb
> of green between the swaying fields
> propels me down into the slack
> lands round the deserted house.

Some of these former rooms and houses, dredged up and grimly refurbished by memory, have the claustrophobic morbidity of Larkin's Mr. Bleaneyland with an extra layer of squalor thrown in. An old flat, for instance, next to the Particular Baptist Chapel:

> It smelt of cat and gas;
> my unmade sheets
> stayed on the bed for weeks ...

This exploration of the past – often a nostalgic past – combined with wit and vivid imagery, occasionally brings to mind the characteristics of the 'Martian' school of poetry (chiefly associated with Craig Raine and Christopher Reid), with its comic and ingenious conceits. Take the poem 'Undergrowth', for instance, written in 1968. It's a witty poem about a middle-aged man coming to terms (or not coming to terms) with his desire for young women. The preoccupation with the injuries caused by time and undiminished desire are neatly pulled together in a phallic joke about Nelson's column:

> Upon his column
> rigid Nelson
> wets his one blind eye
> nostalgically.

A stanza later, the victim of lust and memory who staggers through the poem finds himself in a ruined summer house where

> wasps blaze in a jar
> hung from the warped
> suggestion of a twig ...

That word *blaze* is strikingly right, and once you've been told that's what wasps *do* in a jar, you can't imagine them doing anything else.

In fact, these two particular instances in 'Undergrowth' oddly anticipate some of the effects in Craig Raine's celebrated poem, 'The Onion Memory'. In Raine's tragi-comic poem (in which a divorced couple are wittily but feelingly re-united), there is a rhetorically lush dinner table on which 'the uncooked herrings blink a tearful eye.' When the lovers are walking in a familiar park, mindful of their former passion, 'the old flag blazes on its pole.'

The ingenious wrenching together of extravagant similes, startling images and metaphors which have comic and emotional intensity – these can be found in Robin Skelton's poetry before the vogue for 'Martian' effects acquired fashionable currency. We

come across a scorpion, for example, 'holding her claw like a bible', or an eagle which loftily declares that 'vertigo is my territory'. There is the spider which weaves its webs between the thighs of saints and around the intimate anatomy of the gods with obscene ingenuity:

> I ate flies
> between the lips of her vulva,

and

> I slide my net
> across the coupling buttocks
> of Mars and Venus.

When 'the buzzing of prayers has ended, I scuttle to supper,' the spider nastily confides at the end of the poem. In another poem in Skelton's hair-raising bestiary, there is a bed bug which lies in wait beneath the threshing limbs of a copulating couple before it can feast on them during their post-coital sleep.

The main problem with 'Martian' or 'metaphysical' (in Dryden's denigratory sense of the term) ingenuity is that it can defeat the emotional integrity of the poem and become a mere exercise in cleverness. The balancing act between wit, humour and emotional intensity is difficult to achieve. Skelton brings it off quite wonderfully in a poem called, 'City Varieties, Leeds, 1963'. The poem has metrical calculation and freedom of movement, throwaway humour and elegaic depth. It recalls a performance of 'The Demon Barber' from a theatre bar, where the poet has had a number of meetings with the aptly-named actor, Tod Slaughter:

> He'd run back
> between deaths
> to the Circle Bar for gin.
>
> Jenny was seventy then.
> Was it five hundred
> times, or over a thousand
> he'd done her in?

The poem then moves briskly through a funny recitation of
alcoholic, theatrical and sexual exploits and ends with a fine
metaphysical pun. Despite all the boozey back-slapping and rib-
tickling, the last two stanzas achieve a depth of feeling for the
subject which gives the final joke a sharp edge:

> Dust dries my throat.
> I have another Bass
> on long dead lusts and
> gaieties. No need
> to burlesque their absurdities;
> play them straight,
> walking back from the bar
> into the glow
> of your nostalgia, enter,
> gesture, wait,
>
> and sound the heroic
> statement. Love and Death
> attend the slithering wigs
> and wooden swords.
> The Barber smiles. Time stops.
> His razor lifts.
> And from the Gods we
> thunder daft applause.

The poem ends on a rising note. The humour remains until the
very last line, but the grimace of the skull is there too. Real life and
Victorian melodrama mimic each other and become almost
indistinguishable. The cloak-and-razor progress of the poem is
brought to a high pitch through those slow, heavy, rhythmic
thumps at the end of the penultimate stanza:

> ... enter,
> gesture, wait;

and, again, towards the end of the final stanza:

> The Barber smiles. Time stops.
> His razor lifts.

The effect is funny and majestic at the same time. Despite the
playfulness, this is one of the poems in which Skelton really does
'sound the heroic statement'.

In an analogous manner another poem, 'Sergeant Casey', also opens as a sort of blunt chrysalis, concealing something with a quite different emotional register which is not allowed to hatch out until the end of the poem. The first line has an appealing shock-value:

> Sergeant Casey called them fucking niggers.

What follows, in the first half of the poem, is an apparently straightforward exposition of Sergeant Casey's uncompromising racism. But half-way through the poem, we start to discover that Casey's racism is a form of character armour which buckles in a loathing and dread of suffering itself:

> *Fucking niggers. Wogs.*
> He could not listen,
> fearing the siren music of the damned
> as energetically as he feared the least
> original proposition, or the swollen
> gland, the bloodshot eye ...

The poem turns here, psychologically and rhetorically, from Casey's simple contempt for 'niggers' to the roots of his feelings: Casey isn't let off the hook, but his loathing conceals a buried compassion which is made clear by that sudden rhetorical departure towards 'the siren music of the damned'. His lumpenproletarian single-mindedness is appalling, but Casey himself is appalled by what he sees. The three heavy beats in that phrase, 'least original proposition' (amplified, too, by the discreet way in which it chimes with 'not listen' two lines above), are as ponderous as Sergeant Casey's rigid, redneck attitudes. Rhythm and rhyme effectively underwrite the propositions of the poem itself here. What sounds at first like a high-falutin' abstraction – that 'siren music of the damned' – is effectively grounded in real life by the rhyming echo in that 'swollen *gland*'. These people are damned not by race but by disease and hunger. They are utterly beyond the pale in the eyes of a man who is simple, healthy, and not blessed with anthropological insight:

> I think of Sergeant Casey now, religious
> in his purities, a noble man
> appalled by suffering, knowing it the evil
> pitch he must not touch.

I hear him damn
those torturing fathoms in a sweat-blind rage
of raw humanity and watch him down
his seventh pint,
show snapshots of his children
dancing in the waves on Ventry Strand.

Here, too, there is the heightened rhetoric – 'religious in his purities'; there is the satisfying shift in rhythm – from the staccato stutter of 'sweat-blind rage' to the long beat on the first syllable of 'raw humanity'; there is the tension between the religious purities of Sergeant Casey the 'noble man', and Sergeant Casey the ham-fisted bigot, downing his seventh pint.

There is also an undercurrent which seems to leak unconsciously into this stanza: it starts as a nasty effluvium, but is transformed by the end into something lyrical. That sharp syllabic collusion between 'pitch' and 'touch', which has an immediate tactile force, also half-suggests the sickening pitch and *toss* of a vessel at sea. The man who has been

... certain
of his air and element

and only too

... aware
of all he could not breathe

in the previous stanza, is here drowning in his own loathing. There is a grotesque suggestion that Casey's 'sweat-blind rage' is somehow swelling the 'torturing fathoms'. But immediately after that, Sergeant Casey – homely and human – is downing his seventh pint, and showing

snapshots of his children
dancing in the waves on Ventry Strand.

Thus, the stanza has taken us through a subterranean – or rather sub-aquatic – progression: from the sickening heave in that fourth line, through Sergeant Casey's torturing fathoms, sweat and beer, to the dancing waves in the final line. Sergeant Casey is still Sergeant Casey – blunt and bellicose – but his children will always be dancing in those waves on Ventry Strand, and their dancing confers a sudden grace upon Sergeant Casey himself.

One of the most formally satisfying of all Robin Skelton's poems is 'At Emmet's Grave'. Despite the disclaimer in the opening line, this poem has the monumental weight of the stone it addresses itself to. Quite apart from its sheer technical brilliance, it also works through the simple device of denying what it actually succeeds so well in doing:

> What could be less heroic? Rusted nails
> about a slab of rainswept wrinkled stone,
> bleached white enough, but letterless, unless
> the pocks and seams are script, their language gone,
> forgotten utterly. I watch the stone.
> Who was it said a beauty had been born?

Before the allusions to Yeats's 'Easter 1916' become clear at the end of the stanza, the independent force of the poem has already become firmly established in the first four lines. You already have Emmet's (and Skelton's) stone uppermost in your mind before you're provoked into thinking of the terrible beauty and talismanic stone ('The stone's in the midst of all') in Yeats's poem.

The poem succeeds in doing, through and through, what it claims not to be doing: writing Emmet's epitaph in terms which are modest and heroic at the same time. The conceit is that the poem itself is merely reporting the 'language' which wind and rain have inscribed on the gravestone:

> Hung askew at one end of the rails
> an iron label says half what it means,
> the rest absolved by rust. Undecked by fame,
> here are Robert Emmet, Wind and Rain –
>
> Three Elementals I might say, but that
> such might come near to challenging the ban.
> Let No Man Write My Epitaph. These words,
> if words they are, were written by no man,
> but scribbled out by time and chance alone,
> as if the stone itself would mark the stone
>
> with something to be stared at, questioned, guessed.
> Before the trees made letters maybe this
> was how the sandribs or the troubled pool
> extruded syllables. He could not miss

remembrance any more than in this place
wind can avoid the stone or sodden grass,

Thus the poem manages to accommodate and yet deny Robert
Emmet's famous injunction: 'Let no man write....' While using a
language which is strong, elegaic and formal, the poem presents us
– paradoxically – with a 'language gone'. It yields something akin
to that 'lovely glorious nothing' in Donne's 'Aire and Angels'. We
have a ghostly language which is half there and half not there. This
urges us to reflect on the tragic waywardness of language itself
without allowing us to forget for a moment Emmet's gravestone
'in the midst of all'.

It feels exactly right that the 'language gone' in the first stanza
should half rhyme with the 'wrinkled stone'. For, although the
language has gone, those wrinkles in the stone are a vestigial
language ('the pocks and seams are script'). The whole poem, like
the iron label mentioned in the second stanza, 'says half what it
means', but convinces us, too, that it says everything that can be
said. The dense language is full of echoes which reinforce the
gravity of the poem, sometimes in the manner of half-realized
puns. In the first stanza, the word 'letterless', and the notion of
'letterlessness' are given assonantal and alliterative reinforcement
by the modifier 'unless', which simultaneously introduces the
suggestion that the stone is not letterless at all. In the second
stanza, the 'rest' which is 'absolved by rust' is both the rest of the
message on the iron label, and an oblique echo of the 'rest'
represented by the gravestone itself. There is also that built-in link
between Emmet's own name and the 'elementals' of wind and rain.

There are other places in the poem, too, where assonance,
alliteration, and richness of language lend certain statements an
impressive inevitability: that 'slab of rainswept wrinkled stone',
for example, or the 'extruded syllables' from that 'troubled pool'.
Assonance and alliteration are absolutely dove-tailed here: those
interlocking U's and L's work together to produce a unified effect.
The music of the line is inseparable from its meaning. The pool
extrudes syllables inevitably, it seems; it is a natural process, like
gum oozing from a pine tree or sap from a maple. Furthermore,
the fact that this pool is troubled is what forces the syllables from
it. It is troubled, then, not only in the sense that it is physically
agitated (water in that condition will make sound), but 'troubled'
in the way that the human mind and human language are
troubled, and in the way that Ireland and Robert Emmet are
troubled. Thus the line reflects the whole conceit of the poem.

Let no man write my epitaph, commands Emmet. Yet the epitaph must be written and language is all we've got to write it with. This must have been a fearfully difficult poem to end, but it climbs like a wave to its climax:

> The last offence we practise on the dead
> is how we summarize, for histories need
> what wind and rain supply here, Emmet dead.

Referring to his own poetry, Seamus Heaney (with Anglo-Saxon models in mind) once described the effect he was striving for in terms of 'a grunting consonantal music'. In Skelton's poem, the music is rippling or chiming rather than 'grunting', but the lines roll off the tongue in a way that brings Heaney to mind. Take this line from Heaney's 'The Ministry of Fear', for example:

> Vowels and ideas bandied free
> As the seed-pods blowing off our sycamores

or this one from 'Anahorish':

> *Anahorish,* soft gradient
> of consonant, vowel-meadow,
> after image of lamps
> swung through the yards
> on winter evenings.

Heaney's claim here — like Skelton's — is that the stuff of language (vowels, consonants, syllables, & etc.) is as much a part of the natural world as trees, stones, turf, air and water. To borrow a line from 'Sancreed Churchyard' (which Skelton wrote in 1958), we must learn to 'listen to the great unheard / verbs of the seasons.'

Thus no matter how much craft goes into the making of a poem, and into the manipulation of its language, there is a sense in which the poet also simply takes something from the world around him: from the 'vowel meadow' or the 'verbs of the seasons'. There is a sort of pantheistic muse whose natural function is to extrude syllables and words.

Sometimes poetic 'finds' are quite tangible: the miner's lamp, for example, in a museum in Zennor, Cornwall, which bears the inscription, 'Goodbye the day. Good luck to me.' The line becomes the refrain in Robin Skelton's 'A Ballad of the Mine', one of the most impressive in a group of twelve ballads (reprinted in *Wordsong,* Sono Nis, 1983). Mining disasters have become one of the natural subjects of ballads in the last two hundred years. This one has all the traditional characteristics of the form – the strong hypnotic rhythms, the repetitions, and the percussive alliteration ('daybreak brought the darkness down') – combined with a psychological exploration of the horrible catastrophe which occurred in the Wheal Owles mine at the beginning of the century. The miners accidentally broke through into a flooded mine called 'Come Lucky', and all but one were drowned, and this sole survivor spent the rest of his life as a wandering pedlar:

> we bent to break the clagged ore out
> while breath was harsh as scree
> and sweat slid down the muscled back.
> Goodbye the day. Good luck to me.

The disaster becomes a terrible parody of birth:

> I've never had a dream of what
> the first great morning said
> when the bag of water broke
> for man to breach his head ...

When the wall between the miners and 'Come Lucky' is fatally breached:

> ... The wall of black
> clapped like a Canaanite,
>
> ran like a river down the latch
> and sneck of a deadman's door,
> broke like a bag of thunderclap
> upon the carn-cragged moor.

The sickening, see-saw movement of the verse, the vivid, violent language, and the sheer force of the tale, a tale taken from folk memory – all of these things carry the reader along. Today, in the present climate of relaxed free verse (often relaxed to the point of catatonic slackness), one can hardly think of a form less fashionable than the ballad. But it's form which should be kept alive because it is a bridge between the mandarin end of the poetic spectrum and something which is vital by virtue of its (apparent) simplicity and its rootedness in folk tradition. In any case, as the wide-eyed Mopsa says in *The Winter's Tale*, 'I love a ballad in print ... for then we are sure they are true.'

The kind of poems found in *Limits* (Porcupine's Quill, 1981),

however, are sparse, tight and hard. There are four poems in this
volume which say something about the endeavour behind the
whole collection. The first poem, 'Myself When Young', refers to a
photograph album containing pictures from childhood and the
importance of 'memory's hidden strength'. But the poem
concludes by saying that memory's

> ... richest store
> is in leaving off,
> is in the letting go.

This could be taken as a reference to the necessary leap an
emigrant poet must make in order to embrace a new country.
Perhaps he must embrace a new technique too, for the very next
poem ('The Calligraphy Lesson') begins with the line

> I am learning to write
> again....

A third poem ('The Arrangement'), also begins with the line: 'This
is a new arrangement.' The word 'arrangement', in this case, is
used in the musical sense. The

> Sounds are here
> and here and here

and the poet must learn

> to seize the concerts
> of the air...

The fourth poem ('Something') pulls together all these reflections
on poetic technique, and it needs to be quoted in full:

> Something is hidden
> somewhere and peers out
>
> at the thing called poet
> and his universe
>
> of words and words and words.
> Something is waiting

for the words to stop
so it can be heard

breathing, breathing on
as if breath alone

were the essential
message, words and words

no more than gravel
thrown against the pane.

We've come a long way from the ballad form here – this could be
taken as a virtual affirmation of Black Mountain poetics, with its
faith in breath and visceral wisdom:

breathing, breathing on
as if breath alone
were the essential message.

It's true that these poems have been honed down. Words have
been kept to a minimum. There's a good deal of white space on the
page.
   Despite the fragmented reflections on a new poetics, and the
resolution at the beginning of *Limits* to let go of memory, there
has been a fruitful continuity here between metrical precision,
rhetorical indulgence, wit, and this new desire for sparseness.
There is a lean and remarkable poem, for example, called
'Kinship', which is built around a phonemic pun:

Kin, Kinship, Kindred ...
The look of the words
bothers my head;

that angled beginning,
that whistle-thin
second comer, that *n* ...

That 'n' which occurs in the opening words of the poem is teased
into standing for a doorway and a pair of hooped shoulders, and
then – with a sudden imaginative leap – it becomes:

a stone-hacked hut
the ninth century built

on a dank headland,
a lean shrill child;
and a man with a sword;

it's a scooped cavern
in rotting sandstone
where guns have driven

the sparse survivors
of indian wars ...

The 'n', then, becomes not only an alliterative link between that sequence of things in the poem, but it also functions as a pictograph: the letter itself is made to represent the things it refers to in the mind's eye. The effect of the conceit is that every time the eye encounters that 'n', it becomes an objective correlative for all the things mentioned. The stone-hacked hut, the ninth century, the man with the sword, and those indian wars are disparate and yet related. They accumulate a numinous force, like images from the Tarot.

'When I first set foot on Vancouver Island in 1962, I had a sudden overmastering feeling that I had come home.' That's how Robin Skelton describes what almost sounds like an instantaneous initiation. Although he started to address himself to this new place at once, in the preface to *Landmarks* (1979), he could still say 'only now ... do I feel I have made a true beginning, relating my own present self to the haunting past.' That relationship between the 'haunting past' and the 'present self' has been a source of strength in his poetry: not only has the relationship been a preoccupation in a merely thematic sense, but it has also functioned as a sort of Proustian spur to the making of poems.

It isn't really helpful or necessary to distinguish between the English Skelton and the Canadian Skelton, because many of the poems which have English associations from the past were actually written after he 'came home' to Canada. Also, the *Collected Shorter Poems* contains more Canadian poems than 'English' ones, if such a distinction is made in terms of dates of composition. It's a distinction the book forces readers not to make in any case, because the poems are presented thematically rather than chronologically. 'Sergeant Casey', for example, which has already been commented on, has obvious British associations (the snapshots, the seventh pint, the odour of Imperialism), yet it was written in 1971 – quite some time after Robin Skelton had settled in Canada.

In 'Landmarks', (the title-poem of the 1979 volume of that name), the poet-narrator wanders through the dense BC forest looking for landmarks – and fails to find them. His confused wanderings become a metaphor for a larger kind of migration. Although not mentioned by name, the ghost ships of Cook and Juan de Fuca hover in the mist, greeted by the black canoes of the Indians. The poem invokes the

173

>   solidities
>   of rope and sail
>   and plank and creaking spar

as well as the mariners' journal entries which list

>   the gifts exchanged,
>   the costumes worn, the speeches
>   made.

But the journals

>   do not record
>   that sudden vision,
>   the gasp of miracle
>   and then its loss.

That sudden vision, that gasp of miracle is all too easily replaced by overwhelming agoraphobia. 'I've come too far,' says the wanderer in the poem.

>   Deliberately, I turn.
>   There's nothing here.
>   And nothing comes of nothing.

He is looking for landmarks, mythic centres or gyres, but there aren't any – or at least none that he is capable of recognizing:

>   Can I expect
>   long cabins in a clearing,
>   and a hermit, or a crone,

or perhaps
the remnants of a well
where gold was drowned,
or just incessant forest?

Well, yes, 'log cabins in a clearing' can be expected, but hermits, crones or 'the remnants of a well / where gold was drowned' – these sound more like Celtic mysteries, the mysteries of Penmon Pool in 'The Dark Window'. No 'gyre of form' or 'gnomon of the shell' are found here, but only incessant forest after all. This is no version of Celtic pastoral, but a version of wilderness. Things fall apart, not because the centre cannot hold, but because there *is* no centre. The wanderer is bushed.

'There are no more pain killers,' says one of Samuel Beckett's comic nihilists, and the disoriented wanderer in 'Landmarks' says 'There are no more maps' – only incessant forest. Another wandering figure in the poem, 'O Lazarus', moves through an

emptiness more vast
than any darkness,

and proclaims that he can no longer belong

to any tribe or family
or creed.

Much of Robin Skelton's most recent poetry aspires to a sparse language. It's become honed down to an extent that amounts to a quite deliberate jettisoning of 'rhetoric'. It's certainly true that there are Yeatsian vices in some of the earlier poems. Those particular vices are quite explicit in poems such as 'At Tutankhamun's Tomb, Thinking of Yeats' (1958) and 'Sancreed Churchyard' (written in the same year). They risk going over the top. But it's a risk worth taking, because that impulse to stare the Tradition full in the face produces outstanding poems, such as 'At Emmet's Grave'. Some of the poetry in recent volumes – *Because of Love, Limits*, and *Landmarks* – has been so firmly generated by a desire to jettison rhetorical excess and the vice of 'poetic language', that there is some danger of the very opposite problem: a species of minimalist excess, which can be just as hazardous and seductive as the search for Yeatsian sonorities.

Ordinary language can be made into the most powerful language of all. But it can also remain intransigently ordinary. The metrical craftsman is more aware than anyone else of the muscular effort, the sheer *work,* which is needed to bend the language to his purpose. But if he goes in the other direction and develops an excessively talismanic view of simple, unmediated language, he can start to hear incantation in every syllable. This charge is not one that can be levelled at Robin Skelton, who – despite his allegiance to his own personal species of magic – has resisted cult art and metaphysical theories of prosody. But throughout his work there is a tension between plain statement and the grand style, between the readily 'found' and the consciously made. The poem 'Making', describes this tension in the following terms:

> It is not enough to be wise;
> one must be lucky
> ....
> one must listen,
> as one breathes,
> without selection or knowledge,
> to the only shapes in the air
> that make and echo
> the one particular music
> ....
> structuring the gradual
> language that arrives
> unspoken and complete
> as a phrase of sparstone.

Language may manifest itself like 'shapes in the air'; it may be an aspect of the natural world. But how rarely it arrives 'unspoken and complete'! There's also some casuistical hedging going on here in any case, because the poet who is listening for that language of nature (or language *from* nature) also admits that he must *structure* 'the gradual language that arrives'. What Seamus Heaney calls the 'vowel meadow' and what Robin Skelton calls the 'great unheard verbs of the seasons' are more fully exploited by the poet steeped in craft. That phrase of sparstone may be discovered somewhere in the vowel meadow, but then the sculpting starts.

The issue is directly addressed in the celebrated 'Night Poem, Vancouver Island'. It is a nature poem, full of water, wind and vegetation. There is certainly some 'selection and knowledge' here, but the natural world is asserted to be the 'source' of the poem, and logos comes unbidden from the elemental environment:

> ... logic travelled moss
> upon the hospitable boles

and lichen dribbled song

....

Prayers rot on me like fern

....

a toad stood on the lip of speech
and sang its flies.

Then the narrator-poet comes right out with it: I have forgotten
craft,' he tells us, the implication being that he no longer needs it.
But it's a statement which springs out of poetic license. Indeed, it's
a poetic lie. The craft may be disavowed in the poem, but it isn't
forgotten.

Poems such as 'Sergeant Casey' and 'City Varieties, Leeds,
1963' are not products of labour alone, but nor did they arrive
unspoken and complete. They both validate and invalidate the
serendipity of the vowel meadow. They stand at that
imponderable margin between metrical self-consciousness and the
open plain of free verse. Although Robin Skelton claims to have
merely copied down (another poetic lie) the fading language from
Emmet's gravestone, and wandered – bushed – without maps in
the incessant forest, listen for a moment to how he makes this man
walk aimlessly along the shoreline:

John Arthur walks the tideline-scribbled sand,
having nothing else to do but let things slide,
driftwood, wreckage, weed kicked into mounds,
poked and prodded, taffled and let bide.

You'd think, his tar-smeared rain-stained mac
flapping at every slouched lunge of the knee,
he had a wisdom that we strangers lack,
some slow-tongued gnomon of sand, wind, and sea ...

and you'd be wrong all through, because John Arthur
has nothing else to do but let things slide;
driftwood and sunlight, weed and wanting, slither
endlessly through him like the sour brown tide,

and days are just for filling in with time.
Get closer and you'll see his sandblind stare.
One foot drags, one hand twitches, waves crash down
and mile and mile on mile destroy the shore.

John Arthur may hang loose, but the poem in which he lives is as tight as a drum, and the shoreline on which he lets things slide is as finely drawn as an Ordnance Survey chart. It's also hypnotic and sensuously alive. After many mapless expeditions of his own, this is the terrain – metrically speaking – to which Robin Skelton has returned.

His recently published translations of the great Hungarian poet, George Faludy, (*Selected Poems* 1933-1980) are a joint victory for both Faludy and Skelton. The life and works of George Faludy have been so richly disrupted by the crises and ideological cross-currents of twentieth-century history that they sound preposterously fictional. So much so, that if George Faludy had not existed he could not have been invented (even by his translator!). For George Faludy has written poems while wandering or being pursued through a dozen countries. They are, therefore, full of the innumerable versions of the haunting past and the present selves which make up George Faludy's personality. The poems are funny, gloomy, heroic, and political. They are about erotic love, science, urban collapse, Michelangelo, Milton, Hitler, Plato, the Secret Police, the fate of Hungary and Tibet, the North African desert, the concrete utopia of Toronto, and other things besides. Formally, the poems are tightly crafted and metrical. They are also thoroughly modern, having germinated into consciousness through the rigours of fascism and communism, imprisonment, and picaresque circumstances. Together, George Faludy and Robin Skelton have played the grand things straight. Skelton has brought Faludy alive for English-speaking readers, and Faludy has provided Skelton with a means of demonstrating that his own metrical powers are anything but forgotten.

George Faludy at 75 still looks and sounds like a man full of life. If Robin Skelton – recently turned sixty – is taking stock and wondering what the future holds, the evidence suggests that it holds a great deal.

George Faludy
Skelton as Translator

ALTHOUGH I ARRIVED LATE on the Canadian literary scene, I had years earlier found, on my son's bookshelf in England, Robin Skelton's excellent edition of Byron and had read many of his poems. Recognizing him to be a first-rate poet, I realized before our first meeting, some years ago, that there could be no reciprocity: Robin could not have read my poems since almost nothing had been translated by then. As a result, I was visited by my customary complexes of inferiority.

Robin's appearance put me instantly at ease. A man of imposing stature, broad shouldered, he wore a more than casual garb that carried numerous vestiges of male fashion since the time of the Empire. Around his neck hung a medal larger than those the hippies used to wear; it might have been a witches' emblem, a plaque of a Hexenmeister, St. Lucy's pentagram, the sign of an ancient pub or even a part of its furniture, or a magic device – I still have not found out. All this was at once modern and medieval, while his staff, the very big, black hat he wore and his broad beard – the end of which bent forward sympathetically, reaching out toward me like that of an itinerant philosopher – together conjured up classical antiquity. His life-loving laughter reminded me of Renaissance laughter, the laughter of François Rabelais, so rare in our world where even the Voltairean smile has left us for good. Sitting down with Robin, I closed my eyes and heard a robin's song.

I hope I may be forgiven for trying to capture the charm of Robin's presence before attempting to say a few words about him as a translator, while I have to leave it to others to honour the different aspects of Robin's many-sided personality. To translate poems into English, and to do it well, has become in the twentieth century a highly complex operation. In my little library, I possess twenty-seven volumes of poetry in English translation published during the last two decades, mostly by Penguin. Nearly all of them contain lengthy prefaces lamenting the impossibility of translating poems into English. This point is abundantly illustrated by the translations that follow.

Different methods are used. Some translators are old-fashioned; that is, with their love for jarring rhymes they prefer to anglicize the metre of the original rather than to translate the poem itself, like Michie's *Catullus*, the *Song of Roland* or Dante's *Vita Nova*.

More 'modern' translators (like those of the *Penguin Book of Chinese Verse*) choose only poems expressing banalities and, furthermore, cut their text gratuitously into declamatory lines which are too flat even to be read aloud. Other translators merely render the poems into uninspired prose (i.e. *Gilgamesh,* Virgil's *Pastoral Poems,* etc.). To understand the impact of such translations, one might imagine Leontine Price distributing copies of a libretto to ticket-holders instead of singing it.

Given these difficulties, what, then, is the explanation for the success of Robin's *Two Hundred Poems From the Greek Anthology,* when even Kenneth Rexroth's versions of the Anthology proved a total failure? It seems that the lyricism of the Greek Anthology can be translated neither by the conservatives' lust for bad rhymes and by their rape of syntax, nor by the linguistic sterility and limping vulgarism of the pseudo-moderns. Robin's genius has built something like an arch over the heads of both these schools by translating, as a poet should do, instinctively, while others rammed their version into the straight-jacket of some premeditated hypothesis. He has conjured up the Hellenic poets in their native towns or, whenever necessary, carried them, across time and space, to our cities. Robin's translation is not an exercise but an adventure which results in a charming and entertaining book that abounds in lyricism, wit, satire and humour. One would wish that Skelton might translate three hundred more poems from the Anthology, as he is robust enough to do it.

Young literatures are seldom interested in the literary achievements of other nations. And even English and American poets have rarely occupied themselves in the past with anything coming from Czechoslovakia, Hungary, Poland or Roumania. I feel myself fortunate to have witnessed the emerging Canadian interest in the poetry of Eastern Europe. Although I would like to mention here John R. Colombo, who was instrumental in this new interest, to look for all the reasons for this trend would lead me much too far. Certainly, it seems that the presence in Canada of emigrants from those Eastern European countries, together with Canadian multiculturalism, must have been influential. Much more decisive, however, was the attitude of Canadian poets who translated the works of their emigrant colleagues with fetching enthusiasm and without the prospect of any reward. This has been going on throughout the past decade.

Meanwhile, Robin has translated nearly one hundred of my poems. It is unnecessary to say how hard it must be to translate from a Finno-Ugric or Altaic-Turkic language – it has not yet been decided into which category Hungarian falls – into an Indo-European language with a totally different linguistic structure. It must be as difficult as to translate from Chinese, but there is a long tradition as to how to translate from Chinese into English. But even more than the difficulty of the translation itself, I want to emphasize the extraordinary nature of Robin's gift to me. He sacrificed a year of his own creative life and, with unremitting enthusiasm, spent it translating my work. I feel ashamed, since he necessarily must imagine me to be a better poet than I am, otherwise he could not have done the job.

We have become so much bound together by friendship and by the drift of the translation that I hesitate here to praise with my own words Robin's magnificent versions since in doing so I hardly can escape the charge of becoming self-adulatory as well. It seems more appropriate to quote the reader from the Georgia University Press (our American publisher) who wrote in his report:

> Mr. Skelton's translations (I should say 'versions' because his work transcends the genre of translation; his poems are much more than translations) evoke the *spirit* of the original and, at the same time, are true to them. The few places where he diverges from the Faludy poems are done with reason – to hit upon the exact American poetic equivalent and not merely a linguistic one.

The reader then enumerates the translated poems he especially holds in esteem: nearly half of them.

During the year-long process of translation, I sent four to six cribs with commentary to Robin every two weeks and he mailed me back the translations from Victoria. I would then try to find passages which had gone slightly off the text. These Robin would correct with unflagging skill and patience. Since I felt that his job was too difficult and mine too easy, I wrote him long letters. They had nothing to do with the translations. In them I described scenes from my life with gusto, hoping to amuse Robin so that he might not become bored with my poesy. Then something happened that I found most elating. Once, in New York, a first class painter had worked on my portrait. As the work progressed, he allowed me an occasional look at it. Gradually I realized that he had not only depicted my face but had also grabbed my character. The realization left me sweating like a horse, though my sweat was warm, not cold, and by no means unpleasant. I felt something similar as more and more translations arrived from Victoria. Not only had Robin grabbed me like the painter, he had also done something the latter could not have done: he had lifted me over the prison-wall of the Hungarian language that I never hoped to scale and had put me down in the West.

This little, erratic sketch was written in honour of Robin Skelton's sixtieth birthday. What I wish him can be expressed in a single word: it is an abstract notion that cannot be defined but that has for everybody a slightly different, though absolutely concrete, meaning; an abstraction that does not lead, like most do, to other abstractions but is an end in itself, the bull's eye of life, advocated by all Greek philosophers and accepted, not without resistance, even by Christendom – namely, happiness.

Sam Hamill
Friend

LIKE MOST OF his readership south of the border, I was introduced to Robin Skelton through his editing; first, through *The Malahat Review,* and then through that extraordinary little anthology, *Five Poets of the Pacific Northwest.* Later, I came to read his translations from the Greek Anthology, his own poetry and prose, and, eventually, his wonderful invention, Georges Zuk.

He has long been a passionate spokesman for poetry and a constant advocate for younger writers. It is an honour to bow to Robin Skelton on the sixtieth anniversary of his birth.

I offer him a poem, 'Friend', composed for another old friend I rarely see, but a poem I could have written for Robin as well.

Friend

It's barely October, but almost
over night, it's autumn.

A few lank strands of sunlight
dangle through the clouds.

The hawks stopped circling meadows
and moved toward trees where varmints nest,

building secret places for the winter.
The days grow fainter, and shadows last forever.

I would like to sit outside today,
to drag my rocker out to the deck and sit

and listen to your stories.
I would like to sit outside in my rocker

and pour you a glass of bourbon.
See, back in that corner,

in the shadows of the cedar,
you see that small Jap maple?

It turned yellow and red last Tuesday.
Monday, it was vermilion.

I love that goddamned tree. Autumn here
is otherwise so subtle.

But good storytelling weather – cool
enough in the evening to enjoy a little fire,

a morning chill
to stir the blood to labor.

Oh, it's not the sun I worship,
but the hour. For now, sit here.

It is a kindness when
old friends can be together, quiet.

This fine October air is ours,
friend, to share. Contemplation

is both our gentlest and
our most awesome power.

Kathleen Raine
Two Autumn Poems

for my old friend Robin Skelton

World, what have you done
With all those dear
Women and men
We have loved and known? Where
Are their voices, none
Like any other? Time
Mysterious imperceptible flowing of now,
Where are they hidden? They were
Here, as we are, real
In the present, the Presence,
Human and warm, familiar –
Where is the once and for ever, and how
Can we reach them there
In the timeless ever
Being of all that they were,
Are, and will be for ever?

                    * * *

A small matter
Whether I hope
To be blessed, or despair
With the lost, on the last
Or any day –

Enough to be
Part and particle
Of the whole
Wonder and scope
Of this glory.

Cannot even
The condemned rejoice
That the Presence is
And is just?

George Johnston
For Robin's Sixtieth Birthday

When I get to Heaven
whom shall I say I know?

Robin Skelton,
wizard of the measured line.

Under a big hat
among whiskers

someone wise
and generous.

Skelton? Ah, yes!
But does he know you?

I preen myself
and smile.

'Perpetual Motion', pen and ink by Graeme Gibson.

Margaret Atwood
Floreat Skeltonus

Robin looks like an irascible owl,
Or like someone who ought to be wearing a cowl;
His habit is tweedy,
His beard somewhat weedy,
But his metres mnemonic
Are truly symphonic,
And his charms, whether muttered or herbal or stinking,
Will fix your arthritis as quickly as winking.
(But slight the West Coast, and your head he'll be shrinking!)
He talks with the dead, as all good poets do,
And will help you concoct your own poetry stew;
His giggle is much like the hiss of a kettle;
Watch out though, his mind's like a trap made of metal.
But is he a Druid disguised as a bear,
Or a bear as a Druid? One has to declare
It's anyone's guess. The main thing is, he's *there*.

Norman Nicholson
This Should Have Been a Poem

DEAR ROBIN,

Skelton, as perhaps not everyone in Canada may know, is the name of a village in Cumberland – Old English *scylf-tun*, the homestead by the shelf. 'Shelf' seems to refer to the ridge of low upland, along the 700 to 800 foot contour, where the higher fells of the Lake District begin to ease down to the Carlisle Plain. On the one side, then, the village has rich agricultural country; on the other, the sprawling moors and poor pastures, empty even of tourists, that lie just to the north of the Lake District National Park.

In its self-contained, unobtrusive, yet thoroughly determined way, it is typical of the four or five villages stretched out between the River Eden and the Cumbrian coast. But Skelton has one quite unusual feature. Half a mile or so from the village, where the land is beginning to heave up again from the valley floor, there stand the pylons and aerials of a BBC broadcasting station. It has been used for many purposes, including – I suspect – matters military or naval, but its main job is to relay radio programmes to the people of North Cumberland. World news, Cumbrian news, gale warnings, market prices for farmers, even announcements of births in the local maternity hospitals. For the most part, it is received only by local people, but I like to think that, by some atmospheric freak, it may be picked up, now and then, by a crofter in the Hebrides, a fisherman in Shetland, or even by some Arctic explorer, high up among the northern ice.

Likewise, Robin, standing as high above most of us as those radio masts stand above the village, you send out your messages to the community round you. I'm sure, too, that your words sometimes reach faraway places and lonely men like me, bringing news, warnings, valuations and announcements of renewed life. It is poets like you who help us to keep in touch.

This should have been a poem, too, but the wind rarely blows through the old thorns now. The thorns still stubbornly persist, however, and I break off a sprig to send you greetings on your sixtieth birthday, from the county of *scylf-tun*.

And, of course, from me.

Seán Virgo
A Reel for Robin

Interior
A narrow classroom, a long table. Against the window, so backlit
by the October sun that his features are indistinct, a man stands,
talking, gesturing.
Follow the pale hands, weaving through his words, webbed by the
sunlight.
He says that poetry is magic, is naming, is a game, a sport, a
hopscotch through the grid of language and possibility. Comes out
of myth, the Bible, Faust.
Says that spells and charms are its roots.

Cut to
Students' faces across the table. My face, a few years older than
the others', watching as much as listening.
His voice recites a dirty limerick, to illustrate a metrical device.

Cut to
His hands, shaping thoughts and instances in the light.
Laughter.
He is quoting Sir Thomas Wyatt: *Into a straunge fashion of
forsaking ...*

Cut to
My eyes.

Cut to
His hands.
He says it must always mean more than it says.

Cut to
My hands, the pad of paper in front of me.
I write:

THEY ARE MERLIN'S HANDS

Cut to
His figure against the light.
He is laughing.

Dissolve
Black and white. England 1931. A man and a woman, dressed in dark clothes, going out through a garden gate.
The laugh continues.

Voice over (mine)
THE UPROARIOUS, INDRAWN LAUGH OF A SHY MAN

Laughter fades.

Cut to
The man and the woman close the gate, walk away. A careful space between them.

Cut to
A small boy, short pants, jersey, watching his parents leave.
He steps out from his covert of goldenrod.
He carries a makeshift bow and arrow.
He looks up.
Three jackdaws are whirling and taunting round the chimney of the house.

Cut to
Living room of house on Sinclair Road. Cadboro Bay through the picture window.
Young Nicholas racing electric cars round a track which takes up half the floor. Young Alison kneels with him. Baby Brigid climbs over Sylvia's knees.
Robin in chair against window's light, holding sheaf of poetry manuscript. Mine. Talking, and editing with fountain pen.

YOUR EAR'S FAULTY HERE. A LINE COMES ALIVE
THROUGH INTERNAL VARIATION, NOT THROUGH THE
ABANDONMENT OF THE ESTABLISHED STRESS-PATTERN

The electric cars are colliding, overturning. The children talk loudly. Sylvia rescues Brigid from the figure eight freeway.

Voice over (mine)
THE FIRST REAL POET I KNEW.
THE MOST GENEROUS.

He has put aside my manuscript. Takes up a magazine from the stool by his chair. *The Listener.*

LISTEN TO THIS

He leans forward to read. His face clearly illuminated now. The
familiar wide beard, combed by the fingers of his left hand as he
reads. The first *Crow* poem Ted Hughes published:

> 'NO, NO,' SAID GOD, 'SAY LOVE. NOW TRY IT. LOVE.'
> CROW GAPED, AND A BLUEFLY, A TSETSE, A MOSQUITO,
> ZOOMED OUT AND DOWN
> TO THEIR SUNDRY FLESHPOTS.

Dissolve to
Riverbank by Goldstream, Vancouver Island.
The shallows filled with salmon, spawning, dying, frayed.
A blue heron startles up. Eagles are flying low above the water.

Voice over (Robin's)
> BIRTH AND DEATH ON THE SAME DAY
> BESIDE THE WATERS: ...

Voice fading gradually under natural riverbank sounds.
Robin and I treading through the rocks and underbrush between
cedar trees.

> ... THE DARK WATERS
> UNDER THE MOUNTAINS, THE WILD FIRES
> RUNNING LIKE SYLLABLES FROM TOWN TO TOWN,
> THE FLOWERS IN MYRIADS, THE DARK FACES
> SHINING AND BLESSING UNDER THE COOL STARS.

A fish, still for a moment, after its thrumming drive through the
pool.
Robin walking on alone, towards the rivermouth.
Silhouette.

Voice over (mine)
> DON'T INTERVIEW HIM – HE'S TOO ARTICULATE,
> HE'S A SHAPER, A SHAPE-SHIFTER. HE'LL STEAL
> IT FROM YOU.

His silhouette against the inlet.

Voice over (Robin's)
STONE TROUBLED, TROUBLED OVERMUCH BY STONES,
WALKED FROM TOWER TO TIDE, STOOD WASHED THERE, STOOD
MY OWN SELF'S TOWER

Dissolve to
Black and white. The young boy's face, watching. Cliffs behind
him.

SKIMMED WITH PLEINSONG, ME,
ALONE AND MOULDED, MANY-TONGUED, ONE-VOICED,
CLIMBING A STAIR INSIDE THE SPIRAL SHELL,
(O GHOSTS, REMEMBER), CLIMBED AND CLIMBING STILL.

Dissolve to
Robin in front of half-dressed Christmas tree. The family's annual
ritual. Noise, laughter, Brenda Lee singing *Santa Claus is coming
to town*, loud, on stereo.
Nicholas and Alison in late teens now, Brigid eight years old,
clear-eyed and watching everything.
Decorations spill over the table and carpet.
Sylvia unwraps and holds up to Robin a glass bird, a very old
decoration.
Their eyes meet, hands touch, as he takes it.

Cut to
A Toronto nightclub basement. A book-launching; my first
collection of short stories.
Robin spills in from the night and the rain, Odin-hatted, cane-
wielding, uproarious, shy.
His eyes seek me out, his arms extend.

Freeze-frame

Voice over (Robin's)
TO YOU I DRINK. THE NATIONS FIGHT
LIKE CHILDREN OVER BRICKS.
POSSESSION IS THE POWER TO GIVE
WHAT YOUR OWN NEIGHBOUR LACKS.
AND LACK IS YOUR OWN NEIGHBOUR'S GIFT
TO MAKE TIME'S MEANING TALL.
THE LONELY DRINKER AND THE THIEF

ARE CRUCIFIED BY ALL.

Dissolve to
A witch's altar in Robin's basement.
The touchstones and apparatus of power, fetish, ritual, healing.
The athalme.

Pan slowly to
Robin at nearby table.
Cutting up girlie magazines. Intent.
Scissor-and-pasting in a lightpool from an anglepoise lamp.

Voice over (Robin as Zuk)
    THE PANTIES OF TWENTY-ONE GIRLS
    LIE IN THE CAPACIOUS

    BOTTOM DRAWER OF THE CHEST
    IN NANA'S BEDROOM.

    ZUK IS DERISIVE:
    THIS IS MERELY AMATEUR:

    FORTY-FOUR TYPEWRITER RIBBONS
    HANG IN HIS CLOSET.

    GLOVED HANDS UNDER HER
    NAKED BREASTS, THE COUNTESS

    TILTS HER NIPPLES ...

Voice fades briefly as new

Voice over (mine)
THERE'S NO CONTRADICTION BECAUSE THERE'S NO
INCONGRUITY.
THERE ISN'T A SOLEMN BONE IN HIS BODY ...

Zuk's voice fades up again

    TO BEAT BEHIND THE
    FLYBUTTONS OF THE SOLDIERS.

NANA, REMOVING ONE IRON TIP
FROM HER BRASSIERE

AND TUGGING OFF ONE BOOT
PICKED UP HER SPEAR

THE SERVANT MAIDS OF THE COUNTESS
SCATTERED, SHRIEKING.

BEHIND THE STABLES
THE HAIRY BOAR WENT MAD

Cut to
Robin and me, crouched under the midden at Mill Bay, in filthy weather.
Combing through the clamshell fragments and the sweet black loam. Each holds up to the other what each would dearly like to be an arrowhead, bone-point, treasure.
They're not, of course.
We fall back against the bank, laughing at ourselves.

Cut to
Crowded party, fancy-dress, in Robin's house.
Darktown Strutters' Ball playing loud and scratchy on a 78RPM record.
Robin the DJ by his old phonograph.
He is tugged away to dance by an insistent, laughing girl.
Follow him through the faces, under the paintings which cover the wall, under the plexiglass eye of Jack Kidder's construction above the hearth.
Most of his tribe are there.
The music swells.

Dissolve to
Auditorium in university. Robin reading from a short story. The man who could walk on water.

Cut to
Robin shopping for rings in a Queen Street pawnshop.

Cut to
Robin shopping for books at Nick Drumbolis's store, Letters.

Cut to
Robin in his tan recliner chair, reading from his wonderful
unpublished novel of crisis in a neolithic community. The names!
Me on the couch to his right, making notes.
Sylvia to his left, absorbed.
The three of us and the cats of course, Sam and Chico, and Frodo
the cockapoo mutt, untypically sleeping.
And Johnny Jameson.
The scene in the novel where the refugee from the tribe, the hunter
of love and alteration, shoots a crow.
As reading continues

Dissolve to
Black and white. The young boy, watching his father digging at
the far end of his narrow allotment.
The boy turns away.
A crow flies low, out of an apple tree, along the hedgerow.
The boy raises an air rifle, and shoots.

Cut to
Classroom at UVIC (the same as in the first scene).
A Creative Writing Department meeting.
Lawrence Russell lounges inscrutably in his chair. Cherie Thiessen
is taking notes. Derk Wynand and I share an ashtray, sliding it
across the table alternately.

Sound
Fading in through the realistic ambiance, a scratchy, 78RPM
recording of *Life Gets Tedious Don't It?*
Dave Godfrey is constructing an amazing schematic diagram on
the blackboard as he talks.

Pan to
Robin, intently writing on a sheet of paper in front of him.

Close up
The sheet of paper. Robin's hand at work.
A rococo gallimaufry of doodles that would leave Professor Adler
speechless.

Dissolve to
Interior, Robin's house.
Sylvia at end of table, calligraphying a poem,

Alison, adult now, carrying in a freshly-pulled lithograph.
Brigid holds up a wench's costume for the next Anachronists'
festival.

196 *Sound*
The music, TV sound quality, from the RSC's production of
Nicholas Nickleby.
Frodo wrastles a cow's knuckle-bone around the hearth.
Robin sits, controlling the remote TV switch.
He and I.
And Johnny Jameson.

Cut to TV screen
Garbo in *Ninotchka.*

Cut to
Nicholas Nickleby. 'Didst beat t'schoolmaster?!!'

Cut to
Robert Newton as Long John Silver. *Cut to*
Charles Laughton. The last scene of *The Hunchback of Notre
Dame.*
Linger a little.

Dissolve to
The Skelton's hallway.
The family performing their Candlemas ceremony.
They wait to receive an honoured guest, while Robin recites his
invocation, inviting Bridhe to enter and grace their house for the
year.
As he concludes, Robin approaches and flings open the door.
As his eyes see her, and his arms open

Freeze frame

Voice over (mine)
>   MAKER, MAGICIAN, SHY MAN, DEAR FRIEND,
>   SLAINTE.

'Never wholly believe a book.' RS

Robin Skelton
Then

It seems like yesterday
though years have stiffened
bone and muscle,
greyed the thinning hair,
robbed us of earlier
pleasures and illusions,
and brought us sometimes
almost to our knees,

it seems so near still,
perhaps out of reach
but only, surely,
for a little time,
and time's a little thing,
its yesterday
no farther from today
than is tomorrow.

Robin Skelton
The Exhumation

Earth in an open skull
the spade has turned includes

a small pebble that shines.
Not mica, not fool's gold,

but an ordinary pebble
in the expected skull,

and, digging further, here
are other stones. The soil

is full of pebbles. Some
are round as marbles, some

angular, some scarred,
some of a sort of blue,

some brown, some black. Take up
these pebbles in your hands.

The usual needs our praise.
Do not forget again.

Robin Skelton
Elbows

There are elbows
one will never know,

never see bracing their
sharpness on a table,

never see changing from
smooth to wrinkle to smooth,

never even catch with a
gasp in the ribs,

but there are always
warm familiar elbows

also, bony, plump, pale,
flushed, soft, rough,

to provide one with the
needs one needs,

The changing shapes of need,
the jutting bones.

Robin Skelton
The Reception

She knows who I am.
Her smile is broad,
her handclasp warm.
We must have had a drink
together sometime.
We have not been to bed.
That, at least, I know.
What does she know?

I feel a twinge of
jealousy. Her memory
is so much better than mine,
and, it seems, warm.
Who are her friends?
She isn't with any friends.
Should I know her name,
and did I, ever?

I say *I had better mingle*,
and move away
with an expression I hope
looks like regret.
It well might. I am,
after all, regretful.
I have missed out on
something I haven't missed.

Poems are easier.
I know who I am
for them, in them,
by the third verse at worst,
and even if I'm not
the man I was,
I am almost the man
I'm going to be

before it's over,
if it doesn't stop
midway in career
as now I stop
looking across the room
to see that she
is someone else,
and rather else than someone.

Robin Skelton
The Man Who Forgot Himself

I HAVE a selective memory. Unfortunately, however, I am not in control of the selecting. I mean, I can remember with awful clarity the name of the pet pig that infested my car for two hours of the journey from Sandy Bar to Dogwood Creek, but I cannot remember the name of its owner or why I was going to Dogwood Creek in the first place. I can recall distinctly the colour and nature of the underwear affected by the accommodating lady I met in Winnipeg, but I can't recall the lady herself at all.

This may seem unimportant. After all, I am not writing my autobiography, and if I were it would be as well not to recall either of those two names for fear of a libel suit. On the other hand, it is extremely irritating not to remember the name of one's doctor. The other week, suffering from a particularly painful attack of bursitis – I think it was bursitis – I was obliged to telephone several doctors who lived in my vicinity and who would therefore be likely to have been my selection, in order to discover if there was any record of me on their books, and only yesterday, while attempting to call in the dog, which had strayed, I realized I did not know what name to call and was reduced to whistling hopefully and shouting, 'Come!' Of course, it didn't come, but two other dogs did, and three neighbours. Perhaps my most embarrassing moment of recent times occurred when I answered the doorbell to encounter an elderly lady who greeted me familiarly and came straight in the house as if she was in the habit of doing so. I called my wife and whispered to her as she came out of the kitchen, 'For God's sake, who is it?' 'It's your mother,' she said.

I live a fairly restricted life so this defect of mine does not usually become apparent to people outside my home circle. Indeed, I work at home, for I am a professional book translator, and, mercifully, my memory does not prevent my retaining my knowledge of Russian, German, and Spanish, and I have spoken French since childhood. Nevertheless, it is all extremely frustrating.

I have tried psychiatrists, of course. In fact I have tried five, for I forgot the name of each one as soon as the session was over, and was too embarrassed to ask the receptionist to whom exactly I had just delivered up my account of what little I could remember of my early childhood, while the board outside the building contained so many names it was no help at all. Why didn't I write the names down? Well, after the fifth psychiatrist, which turned out also to be the first one, I did. I put it under 'D' for 'Doctor' in my address book. The following week (I was supposed to have weekly sessions) I found myself in the office of my wife's gynaecologist.

A few months ago I was describing this affliction to a chap I met in a stamp and coin shop. He was looking over old medals and things and I was wondering whether or not to buy a rather flashy set of commemoratives for my son's birthday, and we got to talking. He asked me my son's name and for the life of me I couldn't remember it. 'George,' I said, 'I think, or is it Jerry? I have a tricky memory,' I explained, shuffling a little. 'My wife says I'll forget my own name next.' He looked at me more seriously than the incident really required, and said, 'That's nothing at all compared to my predicament. I sometimes forget myself entirely.' I smiled. 'Don't we all,' I said. 'The other evening I absent-mindedly committed some faux pas at a party – I've forgotten exactly what it was – and my wife whispered in one of those voices that pierce the eardrum like a needle, "You forget yourself!" Sometimes, when I am dragged off to some important gathering and she thinks I may actually enjoy myself, she says, "Now, darling, don't forget who you are!"' He looked at me almost pleadingly. 'But that's exactly what I do,' he said. 'I forget myself. And I don't seem to be able to stop.'

The man behind the counter was looking at us a bit oddly, and I decided that the commemoratives had lost their charm. My companion also seemed uninterested in making a purchase. I said, 'Would you like to join me for a drink?' 'Oh, yes,' he said, 'please.' He sounded curiously intense about it. I wondered just for a moment if he was one of those unfortunates whose wives send them out with no credit cards and only their bus fares in case they fall by the wayside, but when we got into the bar he insisted on getting the first round, and it was clear that he wanted to talk.

'It began when I was a boy,' he said. 'Sometimes at my parents' parties I would stand by myself, not talking to anyone, and sort of drift off. People walked by me as if they couldn't see me, as if I wasn't there. I didn't mind. It was quite pleasant to feel invisible in those circumstances. Then one night someone trod on my toes, and I shouted, and he looked at me as if he was seeing a ghost and said, "I'm sorry. I didn't see you." He must have had a drink or two, because he added in a bewildered sort of way, "You weren't there at all." "I am now," I said, rather grumpily, wondering if my toes were broken. "Yes," he said, "but where the hell did you come from?" and he went away.

'I didn't think too much about it, but a few weeks later the same thing happened. I was only fifteen at the time and boys of fifteen still hold a suspicion that they might be special in some way and have a secret identity nobody knows about, so I was more interested than troubled. Besides, I found out that it only happened if I sort of drifted off in my mind. If I concentrated on looking at people's faces, or told myself that people were looking at me, I was all right. Then came the affair of the school photograph. It was a hot summer day and the process was extremely tedious. The photographer took shot after shot. I sat there on the bench. My mind was, you may say, miles away, and when the prints came out I simply wasn't in the photograph. My parents were cross about it. They looked at the photograph, and the space where I had been sitting, and asked me where I'd got to. I said, "Nowhere." For all I know that may have been the exact truth. After that whenever I had my picture taken I stared at the cameraman so fixedly that it always looked as if I were imbecilic. "He doesn't take a good photograph," my mother would say as she pushed the latest batch of snapshots across the table at afternoon tea parties, and there would be a muddled conversation about what the word "photogenic" meant, and was it true that off-camera Marilyn Monroe looked like nothing at all.

'It went on like this for years. It wasn't a daily occurrence, you understand. Sometimes a couple of months would go by before it happened again, and I would have to remember to take care. As you can imagine, I spent a lot of time alone. It seemed safer. That was when I started my coin collection. It's a solitary hobby – or at least it gave me an excuse to be solitary.

'When I was twenty-two I met this girl. I was working in an office at the time, and she was secretary to one of the sub-managers. It was pleasant work on the whole, and if sometimes people came to see me and found I wasn't there nobody was very much troubled. I suppose they thought I'd gone to the washroom or something. I should explain that I could always see them, could see what was going on, and hear everything. It was just that I wasn't concentrating on it. I was, you might say, detached. It made it a bit tricky sometimes. On one occasion – and only one – I made the mistake of concentrating myself back again when one of my visitors had not quite left the office and he turned round and saw me. I'd heard of eyes popping but I'd never seen it before. He said, "I didn't ... see you...." I said, as briskly as I could, "Well, you see me now!" and he nodded in a dazed fashion and went out. I never did find out why he had dropped in.

'Anyway, to get to this girl. She was really very nice and attractive and quite bright and I was comfortable with her. I can't say I fell madly in love, but I think I loved her. She said she loved me, at any rate, so we got engaged and her parents threw an engagement party. I suppose I must have been under more stress than I appreciated, and stress always brings it on. I was very nervous.' He paused and said, 'I'm nervous now. Keep looking at me,' and I stared at him. His face was wobbling a little, getting sort of foggy round the edges. I stared harder. In fact I glared. He gave a deep sigh. 'Thank you,' he said. 'Well, now you understand.' I rubbed my eyes. I gestured for another drink without taking my eyes off him. 'It's all right,' he said, 'I'm over it. You can relax. But you can imagine what happened at that party. One minute I was there and the next I wasn't. People had only to turn away from me for a second or two and I would be gone. I didn't always know I had gone, either. I would say something, and find that the person I was addressing was just looking through me. He or she couldn't hear me either. What could I do? After it had happened three or four times I locked myself in the loo and cried. I was only twenty-two, remember, and she was a nice girl.

'The marriage didn't come off. I didn't dare face it. Suppose, just as the parson said, "Dost thou take this woman ...," I vanished. Suppose the witnesses found themselves with nothing to witness. I changed my firm and got myself a little office in the back of the building. I locked myself in, which everyone thought eccentric, but I was a good accountant and they didn't want to lose me. When I'd hear a knock I would concentrate like mad, and it worked out pretty well on the whole. I was living alone by then. It made it easier. And I had my coin collection to keep me occupied. It wasn't a bad life. After a bit I got a promotion, but I stuck to my own little office, became the firm's tame eccentric, I guess. My apartment was a bit cramping, so I got a little house. A woman came in twice a week to clean – always on days I was at work, and so there were no problems. Unfortunately, though, since there were no other people in the house I didn't always know if I was – well, here or there. I mean, in my detached condition, I could still function physically – I could be trodden on quite effectively, remember – and I could cook and do my work on my collection and everything. So I may have spent more time not being there than I knew.

'I mustn't give the impression that I was distressed about my problem. They say you can get used to anything, after all. And occasionally, when I was out shopping or just walking the streets, I heard and saw some very odd things. Quite embarrassing sometimes. If I'd had a sense of humour I could have played some terrible practical jokes, but that's not my temperament. I've always been rather shy and retiring.'

I nodded. I said, 'It does make one withdraw a little – that kind of thing. I mean, I don't go out much myself. It embarrasses people when I forget their names, or who they are, and last month when my wife was away I forgot exactly where I was supposed to be addressing a literary group on "The Art of Translation", and made a guess and got it wrong and found myself at the annual general meeting of the local branch of Alcoholics Anonymous. What made it worse was I was wearing a button that said "Guinness is Good for You".' He smiled sadly. 'I would just have vanished,' he said, 'automatically. I mean, even without intending to. I never do actually intend to, you know. It's not something I want to do. Ever.' 'We're both in a bit of a pickle,' I said. 'Funny we should meet like this. It seems we both are what you might call forgetful.' He took a deep breath. 'It wasn't really an accident,' he confided. 'I followed you into the coin shop. You see, earlier today, when you were in the post office making out that customs form I saw you looking at your driver's licence to find out your own name and address, and I realized we had something in common.' 'I didn't see you,' I said. 'No,' he said, 'you wouldn't have. I followed you down the street,' he said, 'and you went into Eaton's and ...' I think I blushed. I'm sure I should have done. 'I forgot where I was,' I said. 'It was, well, just absent-mindedness.' 'Yes,' he said, and then, 'do you think we could be friends?'

Well, we became friends. I used to visit him regularly one or two evenings a week and sometimes, if my wife had nothing else planned, we would spend Sunday afternoons together. He got quite used to my forgetfulness, and after a time, when he disappeared in the middle of a conversation I would just go on talking as if he were there – which of course he almost was. We really became quite intimate. I'm sure it did us both a lot of good. We didn't have to be on guard with each other at all. I even got interested in his coin collection. About the middle of last year, though, I did have a nasty shock. I went round on a Wednesday evening – I think it was a Wednesday, it could have been Friday – and let myself in as usual, but he was nowhere around. I waited a while, fixed myself a drink, read his coin magazine, and, after an hour or so, I went home. He phoned me the next day apologetically. 'I was there,' he said, 'I was actually there, but something happened. I couldn't *do* anything. It wasn't like usual. I wanted to fix you a drink, and my hand just went through the bottle. I've had a touch of flu. That may have done it. Do forgive me.' I forgave him, of course, but I was worried. I said so to my wife. I said, 'I'm really bothered about what's-his-name. He seems a bit off colour. Maybe I should go round.' 'Do you remember the address?' she enquired, really very sensibly. 'I have it in my book,' I told her proudly, and showed her the entry, 'The Man Who Forgets Himself', and his address and phone number. 'Why "The Man Who Forgets Himself"?' she said. 'I thought that described you!' 'We have similar problems,' I told her. 'That's the bond between us.' My wife sniffed. She is really a very good woman and an admirable wife, but she does sometimes sniff a little.

I went around straight away, of course, and there he was, quite happy to see me and altogether his usual self. He didn't disappear all evening, and even seemed cheerful about the effects of the flu. 'It was strange,' he said. 'You know, I couldn't get myself a single thing to eat or drink, but I didn't seem to need it. I know that people on hunger strikes have to have liquids, but I got on just fine without anything. I could go on like that forever, maybe, though if I got sick it might be a problem. Maybe not, though. I mean, if you're not there how can the viruses find you?'

I nodded wisely. I thought he was a bit over-excited. Whether or not the flu was the cause, the same thing happened a couple of weeks later. Somehow I'd expected it. I sat around, gave myself a drink and, feeling a bit foolish, for he might simply have gone out for the evening, I talked to what seemed empty air, told him what gossip there was to tell, and so forth. The next time I called he told me I'd been quite correct. He'd been there all the time, completely detached he said; in fact, he'd been completely detached for three days.

I was a bit alarmed, but he was quite cheerful about it. He was even more cheerful the next time I called. He showed me a magazine – I forget the name – with an article in it about people who suffer from 'Complete Psychical Withdrawal' combined with something called 'Astral Travel' and 'Loss of Physical Entity'. It was something like that anyway. It was put out by some foundation that was pursuing parapsychological research, and it looked very scholarly and reliable. You could tell from the footnotes. 'They're doing some tests in this clinic in Switzerland,' he said. 'I have the time, now I've retired, and so I'm going over there to see what's what. I phoned them and they seemed very helpful and quite willing for me to pay them a visit. I didn't tell them too much, of course; they might have thought I was crazy. I just said I'd read the article and seemed to have some of the symptoms. Anyway, I got the tickets today and I'm leaving tomorrow for a month. Wish me luck!' I wished him luck. He said, 'I suppose you couldn't come along?' but I had to say I couldn't afford it. He said, 'Can I ask you a favour? I wonder if you'd look after the house while I'm gone.' He hesitated. 'If anything ... happens ...' he said, 'you'll find some papers in the desk drawer upstairs. Try to remember.' I said I'd remember, and I wrote it down in my book.

I looked after the house as well as I could, and I spent a good deal of time browsing over the coin collection. I'd hoped for postcards, but none arrived. After the month was up I expected him daily, but he didn't turn up. Indeed, the only person who did turn up was a niece I didn't know he had. She showed me a letter he had written. It said that if he didn't return by the end of the year the house and its contents, apart from the coin collection, were hers. The coin collection, he said, was to come to me. The necessary papers were in the desk upstairs. It was December by that time, so we both went upstairs and, sure enough, there were the papers. It was all in order: two deeds of gift. 'It's odd,' said the niece. 'What do you suppose could have happened to him?' I said I didn't know, but he'd always been a very original man.

The niece didn't sell the house. She moved into it. We became good friends. I used to visit a lot and whenever I could manage it I'd arrange to be alone in the house for a while, and I'd just sit there in his chair and talk to what seemed like empty air. It made me feel good to do that in the way I'd done it so often before. I didn't like to tell the niece that I had found the ticket to Switzerland, unused, in the little secret drawer of his desk. I didn't want to go into all that. It would only have upset her, and, besides, she would certainly have asked me the name of the clinic, and, naturally, I have forgotten.

Robin Skelton
Incomplete

I REALLY DON'T KNOW why you're questioning me, unless it's just
to keep in practice. One must keep in practice, I suppose. I'll tell
you my name, shall I? It is Henry, Henry Quill. No middle initial. I
was always being asked about that, right from boyhood, and all
the forms you have to fill in have a space for a middle initial. But I
didn't – I don't – have one. It sometimes made me feel a little
incomplete.

Perhaps that was the cause of the trouble, if you can call it
trouble. I didn't always think of it that way. Sometimes I felt sort
of proud. But you don't know what I'm talking about, do you?
Well, to put it as plainly as I can, I could never really finish
anything – and I suppose I still can't. When I was small and
making things – paper aeroplanes even, and, later, rabbit hutches
and model ships, I somehow always stopped before the things
were completed. Perhaps I felt it was more blessed to journey than
to arrive, I don't know. I think, actually, it was more that I saw it
all finished, had it in my mind so to speak, and there seemed no
point in taking a step that had already been taken. That was when
I was young. Later on it was maybe a bit different. I developed a
little ambition, not very much, but enough to get me through
examinations, though I almost never finished the papers. Still,
that's not unusual. There's never enough time to finish an
examination, so perhaps that doesn't count. I even got my degree,
though that was a bit of an accident. I'd miscounted the number of
credits I needed and I never did need to pass that last course, so
missing the examination had no effect at all.

I don't want you to think I was lazy, or even incompetent. I
loved starting things. Goodness, how many things I started! You'd
be astonished. I remember beginning a society for the planting of
trees in public places. It had a constitution and everything. Of
course I didn't actually plant any trees myself, but when I turned
to something else the other members took it over, so it didn't
matter. Societies are good in that way. There's always somebody
else. I can't remember how many groups, societies, and dinner
clubs I began. I was very sociable in those days. Popular, too.
People liked me because I was always coming up with new ideas –
new then, of course. You'd think them pretty old hat now, I guess.

Work? Well, I had a little money so I didn't have to take a real
job, not regularly at least. I did a little of this and that. I was good

at interviews. They liked my ideas, but somehow I never stayed very long. I wasn't much of a stayer. That's what they used to say about me, of course. 'Henry's very bright, but he isn't a stayer.' I heard it a lot of times in corridors and washrooms when they didn't know I was in a cubicle. Mind you, I wasn't idle. Far from it. I was always busy. I wrote books. Yes, I know, you won't have heard of them, but some of them were quite popular in their time. I would slog away at the typewriter for months. I never actually completed one myself, though. I mean I was the author all right, but I just couldn't face making that final series of revisions, or sometimes even writing that last chapter. My wife saved me there. She really should have had her name on the title page as well as mine. She did the revisions for me, and sometimes she even wrote the last pages. You couldn't tell, though. She knew my style perfectly. It made it easy for me. Right from the beginning I knew that I didn't really have to finish it. Of course I intended to; I always intended to. 'This time,' I would tell myself, 'I'll get it right to the end.'

That word 'end' often did me in, for all my good intentions. It seemed so final, like a little death. I could never write the word, and when I saw it coming up on the cinema screen or on the last page of a book, I avoided looking at it. I felt somehow that things weren't supposed to end, that there should be no end to anything. I never went to funerals, and I left concerts before the national anthem. They always played the national anthem to finish up with in those days.

You want to know about my wife? Well, she understood me. I've heard cynics say that there are two great disasters for a married man: one is to have a wife who doesn't understand him and the other is to have a wife who does. It wasn't like that for me. I was grateful. I was grateful from the very start when I began to propose to her in my bachelor apartment on the big sofa with the loose springs. I was re-upholstering it, but I hadn't quite finished. I said something like, 'There's a question I've been wanting to ask you for a long time.' She said, 'Yes?' and smiled at me, and I froze up. I managed at last to say again, in a sort of choked voice, 'for a long time.' She put her hand on mine and said, 'Of course I will marry you,' and there we were. The marriage ceremony was a bit tricky, but I got through it somehow. I told myself that the wedding would not be completed until we'd signed the book in the vestry and that got me over the 'I do' bit of the service. Then in the vestry I told myself that a marriage wasn't a complete marriage until it had been consummated. Those were the days when people

believed in things like premarital chastity. In bed that night I was
very tense, but, as I say, she understood me. She told me very
gently, 'Darling, this is a beginning. There's so much ahead. Just
think of all the years, and happiness to come. And the children.
They say it's the first child that really sets the seal on a marriage.'
We never did have any children.

It was a happy time mostly. I wrote – or almost wrote – books
in between spells of work with one firm or another; I arranged for
my lawyer to sign the contracts; I couldn't face that myself. My
wife handled the bills. They upset me. Especially when I had
delayed paying them and got a piece of paper with 'Final Demand'
printed on it. I did odd jobs around the house, too. I enjoyed that.
I was good with my hands in those days, and my wife became a
really efficient carpenter, so she could finish whatever I had begun.
Oh, I didn't just begin projects and abandon them; I had to get
them almost to completion. Once or twice I accidentally finished
something. I found that alarming. I would sit and stare at the
repaired table, or the re-upholstered chair, and my wife would
have to come to my rescue. 'There's just one thing you haven't
done, dear,' she'd say, and she'd point to a scratch or a missing
upholstery nail or something like that. I rather think that on
occasion she made the scratch herself or pulled out a nail when I
wasn't looking.

All right, I know what you're thinking. Why didn't he take his
neurosis to a psychiatrist? Well, honestly, I didn't see any reason
to. We had a good marriage, you know, and we were always
working together. If I'd been cured – I suppose I have to concede
that my condition might be thought an illness – it would have
broken a kind of bond between us. So we went on together very
happily.

I don't much like to remember what happened next. It was just
after Christmas and I was a bit depressed. The last day of the year
was close and I was always depressed at that time. My wife was
out of sorts too. Just out of sorts. Nothing serious. Or so I thought
at the time. Still, I made her stay in bed and brought her breakfast.
I remember that I hadn't buttered the toast. Well, she got worse,
so I called in the doctor. I suppose it must have happened to
hundreds of people, but it was inconceivable that it could happen
to me. She went into hospital and it was only a matter of weeks.
Three weeks, as I recall. I visited her regularly and she was very
brave about it. She knew, of course. She was a wonderfully
intelligent and sensitive woman. The last day I saw her she said to
me, 'I'm going, you know. I hope you can manage. Get someone

else to handle the bills. Think of it as a beginning,' but I found it hard to do that. 'What beginning?' I asked. 'You're beginning a new life,' she said '– and me too probably.' She didn't sound too certain, and I wasn't certain at all.

I wasn't there at the end. I couldn't manage it. I am sure she understood. I did get to the funeral. There was no escape. She had relatives, you see. But when it came to 'Ashes to Ashes and Dust to Dust' I'm afraid I just turned around and ran. Yes, literally. I ran from that graveyard. People were kind about it. They said, 'You were overcome. It was natural. You couldn't face it.' They didn't really understand what it was that I couldn't face, but she would have understood.

Life was difficult after that. I couldn't come to grips with things. I saw no point in beginning another book. There was no one to finish it. I cooked for myself, but it was never satisfactory. I always left something out. I thought of suicide, but it seemed so, well, final. At last, though, I came to a point when I knew I would have to make the effort. I put my head in the gas oven first. It seemed an easy way to go. But the gas made me cough and I couldn't go on with it. I thought of poison next, of taking an overdose of valium with whisky; I reckoned that should be painless as well as efficient, but at the last minute, when I was beginning to feel drowsy, I rushed to the bathroom and abandoned the idea. I was very upset by that time. I wanted to do it, you see. I wanted, at last, to complete something, even if it was my own life. I tried becoming accident-prone. I walked across the street in the middle of traffic. I was cursed but not killed. I hired a drunk man to take me out in a boat when the seas were high, and I survived. The whole of my life became concentrated upon how exactly I could manage to leave it. I became ill, I suppose with the worry of it all, but illness was no solution. I had to do it myself. I had, as they say, to finish myself off.

At last I managed to talk myself into it. I told myself that death was not the end. I told myself it was simply a change, a movement onward, a beginning. I said, 'You have always begun things. You must begin this!' and one day I got a gun from the shop downtown and some ammunition and I went into the living room – this room – and put the muzzle – I think they call it a muzzle – into my mouth and said out loud, though my voice was a bit muffled because of the muzzle, 'This is how it begins,' and I pulled the trigger.

I should have known better. They found my body the next day and said I was dead. They said I had met my end. But I hadn't, you see. You of all people, round this table with the candles and the crystal ball and all, will understand that. I hadn't ended at all. I was still there – or here, if you prefer. And I keep on saying to myself, 'When will it end, when will it ever end?' and I don't want it to, you know. I don't even like asking the question. It's ridiculous, I know it's ridiculous, and I am rather ridiculous myself, but there is so much more to say before it's over. There is so much more to say....

Robin Skelton
The Barrens

(Triolets)

Over the wilderness we go,
accepting space and time and death

that alter all we think we know.
Over the wilderness we go,

the ice, the tundra; here below,
trapped in the ultimate of breath,

over the wilderness we go,
accepting time and space and death.

We move towards the final chill,
accepting death and time and space

which are the climax of the will;
we move towards the final chill

of every impulse we fulfil
by travelling this emptied place.

We move towards the final chill
accepting death and time and space.

It is the ultimate we serve,
accepting space and time and death,

the distance between nerve and nerve.
It is the ultimate we serve

through love and terror that observe
the chill declensions of the breath.

It is the ultimate we serve,
accepting space and time and death.

Robin Skelton
Prestidigitation

The best tricks are the
easy ones. I turn

from summer into
autumn like a leaf

that's known this all
its life, or like the sun

that shifts its track so
slily you can't say

quite when it happened
though you watched it happen.

The next trick's easier still,
so don't applaud.

Robin Skelton
Haystack Rock

for Sylvia and Brigid

This rock is metaphor; it lifts
up through a band of grey and silver mist
its vast bird-haunted breast as if, once earth
were tilted, sky would nuzzle there to suck.

I trudge towards it, held upon my course
as if it were a lodestone, I the pin.
Ahead, sand is a mirror slick as ice
to teach the clouds to skid, the morning walkers
to slip through the surface to themselves,
and as I cross that shine to steadier sand
I pause at stretchmarks on the tightened skin,
at scars left by the scalpel tracks of birds,
and weals from whips of lost initiations,
and the rock looms closer, closer, till
the sky is almost filled with it and I
am one of many scattering at its base,
men, women, children come there as a tribe
comes to the call from all their scattered creeds,
and wander lonely, mindless, through the crowd.
A crow steps delicately between two pools,
the black head jerking at each printed sign;
a white gull perches on the highest peak,
and, over there, where soon the tide will turn,
two boys bruise knees into a cavern shaped
threefold, a triple aperture in time
and space and breath; I wait for their return,
fearful of depths of darkness; they come back
small as the winking pink in this round pool
I find my feet by. And now, farther up,
I see another tall against the sky
and envy him that careless arrogance
which I have lost, as I have also lost
the way into the cavern and the way
to walk back undisturbed to common shores,

having myself become a metaphor.

Robin Skelton
Personally

Personally, I discover history
first in my bones, then in the bones of the land,
the worn formations which are where we live
separate or together on this island

about which they have written, spacing out
the happenings year by year and day by day,
person by person. I know Juan de Perez
failed to plant the cross five years before
Cook's men fathered unrecorded children
on the lonely Village Of The Wind

for instance, and today I cannot look
upon a cross or walk the sea-stirred island
without this being in me, though I felt
it in me long before I laid the book
upon my table and was told a date
that proved irrelevant, as always time
will prove irrelevant. We are how we've grown
into this place and how the place has grown,
and history is the way we reach our hands
into the past and take it personally.

Biographical Data

1925 Born October 12, the only son of Cyril Frederick William Skelton and Eliza Skelton (née Robins) at the Schoolhouse, Easington, E. Yorks. Right thigh broken at birth, but soon healed.

1934 Began writing verse.

1936 Commenced as boarder at Pocklington Grammar School, near York.

1942 Passed 'School Certificate' examination with distinctions in English and Mathematics, and credits in Geography and French.

1943 Volunteered for the RAF. Became an officer cadet and student at Christ's College, Cambridge, studying Economics, Civics and Politics. Passed academic examinations with a second class. Failed RAF examinations. Member of the Cambridge University 'Mummers'. First poems published.

1944 Entered the RAF proper and commenced training as Flight Engineer. Training of Flight Engineers being suspended, remustered as Code and Cyphers Clerk.

1945 Posted to New Delhi as Code and Cyphers Clerk with the rank of Sergeant. Transferred to 21 Care and Maintenance Company at Samungli, near Quetta.

1946 Visited Ceylon for a month's course of training to become an Educational and Vocational Training Instructor. Returned to England on leave for two months.

1947 Transferred to New Delhi. Wrote scripts and broadcast for the Western Music Division of All India Radio (Station Delhi). Wrote and co-produced the hour-long feature 'Friday the Thirteenth'. Wrote and acted in shortened versions of Restoration comedy. Returned to England and was demobilized. Entered Leeds University as a student of English Language and Literature. Met Geoffrey Keynes.

1949 Became editor of *The Gryphon*. Articles, poems, stories, and drawings published in university magazines. Organized exhibition of twentieth-century book design for the Brotherton Library. Directed plays for the English Society.

1950 Became regular drama critic of the Union News. Edited and published *Leeds University Poetry 1949* (Lotus Press). Bought The Lotus Press from Geoffrey Handley Taylor. Received a first class honours BA in English Language and Literature.

1951 Received MA for thesis on the writings of Francis Quarles (1592-1644). Became an assistant lecturer in the English Department of the University of Manchester. Dissolved The Lotus Press, after publishing seven paperback volumes.

1952 Began helping Geoffrey Keynes in his work on the letters of Rupert Brooke. Lecturer for the Workers' Educational Association and Manchester Extra-Mural Department. In subsequent years, attended and / or organized weekend schools in Lancashire, Yorkshire, Suffolk, Staffordshire, and the Home Counties.

1953 Married Margaret Lambert.

1954 Promoted to lecturer, with tenure. Became an examiner in English literature for the Northern Universities Joint Matriculation Board.

1955 *Patmos* is the Poetry Book Society Choice for the Autumn.

1957 Divorced. Married Sylvia Mary Jarrett on February 4. A son, Nicholas John, born on 4 December. Became regular poetry reviewer for *Books,* (the Journal of the National Book League), and for *The Manchester Guardian.* Organized an exhibition of books, manuscripts, paintings, and photographs relating to twentieth-century poetry for the university's art festival. Founded (with Michael Seward Snow and Tony Connor) 'The Peterloo Group' of poets and painters. Became Chief Examiner in English Literature ('O' Level) for the Northern Universities Joint Matriculation Board. Began making collages.

1958 Ceased work as poetry reviewer for *The Manchester Gaurdian* and became one of its team of drama critics. Began to give broadcasts for the BBC, and was a member of the BBC's 'Fifty-One Society' (a debating society formed of professional men and writers in the North of England, whose proceedings were broadcast regularly from 1951 to 1961). Became Chairman of Examiners in English Literature ('O' Level) for the Northern Universities Joint Matriculation Board.

1959 Lectured to the annual conference of Her Majesty's Inspectors of Schools (Inspectors in English Literature). Prime mover in the creation of a new Examination in English Literature for Secondary Modern Schools for the Northern Universities Joint Matriculation Board. Alison Jane Skelton born on September 27. Wrote the words for two motets and a cantata by the composer David Freedman.

1960 Was founder-member and First Honorary Secretary of the Manchester Institute of Contemporary Arts. Wrote the

constitution of this society, and was chairman of its Programme
Committee for 1960-1962. MICA was responsible for many
poetry readings, lectures, concerts, exhibitions, and literary and
artistic symposia during this period. Gave a series of talks about
poetry on the BBC 'Third Programme'. Became a regular poetry
reviewer for *Critical Quarterly*. Visited Dublin for the first time
and began work on the papers of J.M. Synge.

1961 Organized the book section of the exhibition, 'W.B. Yeats /
Images of a Poet', which was shown in Manchester under the
auspices of Manchester and Reading Universities. Organized
the transportation of the exhibition to Dublin and its showing
there in the summer of the same year. Appointed general editor
of the Oxford University Press edition of *The Works of J.M.
Synge*.

1962 Visited Victoria College, BC to teach summer school.
Appointed to a visiting professorship at the University of
Massachusetts as part of the University's celebration of its
centenary. While in Massachusetts organized a weekly poetry
magazine, *Poetry Circular,* and gave poetry readings and
lectures at Mount Holyoke, University of Massachusetts, and at
Lexington. Also broadcast a poetry reading for an educational
radio network.

1963 Emigrated to Canada and became an associate professor in
the English Department of the University of Victoria, BC.

1964 Became regular art columnist for *The Victoria Daily Times*.
Death of Cyril Skelton.

1965 Organized (with Ann Saddlemyer) the exhibition, 'The
World of W.B. Yeats' and edited the symposium of the same
title. Organized the publication of the symposium and arranged
for the publication of English and American editions by Oxford
University Press and Washington University Press respectively,
in addition to the Canadian edition. Gave a centenary lecture
on the work of W.B. Yeats on the centenary of his birthday in
Dublin. Lectured at the Sligo International Yeats Summer
School. Gave (with Ann Saddlemyer) a series of thirteen talks
on Irish literature for CBC Radio. Gave an additional talk for
another branch of CBC and played the part of W.B. Yeats in an
hour-long radio documentary feature broadcast by CBC in July.
Gave poetry readings in Victoria and in Dublin. Partially
organized and lectured at W.B. Yeats Festival of Portland State
College. Was one of the prime movers in founding a Rare Book
Room at the University of Victoria Library.

1966 Eleanor Brigid Skelton born on 31 July. Promoted to a full professorship with tenure. Began planning *The Malahat Review* with John Peter. Elected a Fellow of the Royal Society of Literature. Organized and lectured at the W.B. Yeats Festival of Central Washington State College, Ellensburg, Washington. First one-man exhibition of collages at Pandora's Box, Victoria. Ceased writing weekly art column for *The Victoria Daily Times*.

1967 First number of *The Malahat Review,* edited by John Peter and Robin Skelton, appeared on January 1st. Taught summer semester as a visiting professor at the University of Michigan, Ann Arbor. Planned a comprehensive creative writing programme for the University of Victoria, and became Director of the Creative Writing division of the English Department. Read a paper at the annual conference of the American Committee on Irish Studies at Hollins College, Virginia.

1968 Second one-man exhibition of collages at the Print Gallery, Victoria. Elected to membership of the board of directors of the Art Gallery of Greater Victoria for 1968-1969. Amateur production of play, 'The Author', in Victoria, BC.

1969 Founded the annual series of anthologies of writings by University of Victoria creative writing students, *Introductions from an Island*. Attended PEN Congress at Menton, France. Visited Italy, Corsica, Switzerland, Ireland, England, during sabbatical leave. Acted as an external examiner for the University of Exeter in connection with an experimental programme of combined English honours and visual arts.

1970 Elected again to membership of the board of directors of the Art Gallery of Greater Victoria for a two-year term. Visited Mallorca for the first time. Returned to Canada on the SS Oriana, calling at Bermuda, Nassau, Florida, Panama, Acapulco and San Francisco. Lectured to the Royal Society of Literature in London.

1971 Presented a paper at the Synge Centennial Conference in Dublin. Revisited Paris. Began making sculpture. Elected vice-president of 'The Limners Society' of Vancouver Island artists. Portrait painted by Myfanwy Pavelic. Organized the creation and presentation of the Michael Dane Memorial Collection of paintings, drawings, and collages to the Art Gallery of Greater Victoria. Portion of Sylvia and Robin Skelton's art collection shown in a special exhibition at the Art Gallery of Greater Victoria. Read and recorded poems at the Library of Congress. Presented a paper on Jack B. Yeats to the Irish Studies Conference in Toronto. Presented a collection of the books, letters, and manuscripts of W.R. Childe to the MacPherson Library of the University of Victoria.

1972 Co-writer and co-director with Bill Thomas of the film 'A Long Road Back', made for the British Columbia Government Committee on Alcohol and Drug Abuse. Founded the Pharos Press. Taught at the Creative Writing Summer School of Eastern Washington State, Cheney, Washington. Gave a poetry reading at the annual conference of CCLMA in Portland, Oregon. Re-elected to the board of directors of the Art Gallery of Greater Victoria for a further two-year term. Visited Robert Graves in Mallorca for the second time. Elected member of the planning committee for a proposed Western Canadian Publishers' Association.

1973 Founding Chairman of the Department of Creative Writing at the University of Victoria. First listed in *Who's Who*.

1974 Received a Canada Council grant for research into the history of the Cariboo area of British Columbia. Lectured at the BC Penitentiary and Matsqui Penal Institution. Exhibited collages and sculptures in a group exhibition of 'The Limners' in Victoria.

1975 Elected to the executive of the Canadian Periodical Publishers' Association. Edited, with Bill Thomas, a special issue of *The Malahat Review* in tribute to Robert Graves on his 80th birthday. Interviewed Robert Graves in Mallorca for the BBC and created a 75-minute feature programme which received the BBC's Best Programme of the Month award. Was the subject of two CBC radio programmes.

1976 Resigned the chairmanship of the Creative Writing Department of the University of Victoria. Became Editor-in-Chief of the Sono Nis Press. Elected a Knight of Mark Twain, filling the position left vacant by the death of C. Day Lewis. Became a Fellow of the English Centre of International PEN. One of three poets representing British Columbia at the Olympic Games. Exhibited collages in a group show of 'The Limners' at the Shaw-Rimmington Gallery in Toronto.

1977 'Landmarks' published in *Poetry* (Chicago). Elected Chairman of the Archives Committee of the Writers' Union of Canada.

1978 Poetry reading tour in Southern California. Reading in Port Angeles, Washington. Collages included in an exhibition of the work of 'The Limners' at the Uttley Galleries. TV Guest Appearance on 'Ninety Minutes Live'. Re-elected Chairman of the Archives Committee of the Writers' Union of Canada.

Travelled in Europe on Canada Council grant, interviewed on television and radio in UK. Read poems on CBC radio. Contributed to the anthology, *Tributaries*.

1979 Poetry readings in Calgary, Penticton, Vancouver. Appeared on the television series 'Canadian Authors'. Served on the committee to review the Creative Writing Department at the University of Victoria.

1980 Made opening speech for Herbert Siebner's exhibition of twenty-five years of painting at the Media Centre, Vancouver. Appeared on the TV programme 'Arts Canada'. Presented report on authors' wills to the AGM of the Writers' Union of Canada. Elected member of Standing Executive Committee of the BC Branch of the Writers' Union of Canada. Appointed BC representative on the Executive Committee of the League of Canadian Poets and founding chairman of the BC branch of the League. Appointed member of the Canada Council Jury for Senior Arts Grants (Writing and Publication Division). Gave poetry readings at York University, Scarborough College, Douglas College, Centennial College, Niagara College, and to the Axletree Group of writers. Attended, by invitation, conference on International Writer Exchange organized by the Ministry of External Affairs in Vancouver.

1981 Elected First Vice Chairman of the Writers' Union of Canada. Elected Chairman of the Constitution Revision Committee of the League of Canadian Poets. Taught creative writing at the Island Mountain School of the Arts in Wells, BC. Gave poetry reading at Harbourfront, Toronto, and was interviewed on CJRT-FM radio in Toronto.

1982 Chairman of Conference on Technology and the Writer held in Toronto by the Writers' Union of Canada, the Canadian Translators' Association, and The Union des Ecrivains de Quebec. Elected Chairman of the Writers' Union of Canada. Attended, by invitation, the 'Night of One Hundred Authors' banquet in Toronto, organized by the Writers' Development Trust. Gave public reading of the poetry of Maxwell Bates at the Art Gallery of Greater Victoria. Taught at the Island Mountain School of the Arts in Wells, BC.

1983 Contributed story to anthology, 'Rainshadow'. Gave reading and seminar at the University of Waterloo. Gave paper on 'The Teaching of Poetry' at 'The Creating Word, An International Conference on the Learning and Teaching of English in the Nineteen Eighties' at the University of Alberta. Together with Susan Musgrave, toured Ireland under the auspices of the Ministry of External Affairs and gave readings, talks, and workshops in Dublin, Limerick, Newcastle West, Waterford, Wexford, Tralee, Listowel, Tuam, Sligo, Westport, Galway and Cork. Appeared on the TV programme 'Focus' in Dublin. Taught at the Island Mountain School of the Arts in Wells, BC. Delivered a paper on 'The Acquisition of Literary Archives' to the 1983 annual meeting of the Association of Canadian Archivists in Vancouver. Elected Chairman of the Membership Committee of the Writers' Union of Canada. One of the judges of the Alberta Poetry Competition. Three-act play, *The Paper Cage* performed at William Head.

1984 Gave reading at Harbourfront, Toronto, and in White Rock, BC. Judged the William Stafford Poetry Competition for the Washington Poetry Association, and gave a seminar and reading at its annual general meeting. Gave readings at four colleges in the Seattle area. Taught advanced poetry writing at Fort San, Saskatchewan, for the Saskatchewan Arts Board. Appointed member of the Arts Advisory Committee of 'Island 86' in Victoria. Gave reading at Sunfest festival in Victoria, and reading-lecture on translating George Faludy at Western Front in Vancouver.

1985 Gave readings of translations of the poetry of George Faludy, together with Faludy himself, in Victoria, Vancouver and Toronto. Spoke, and read poem, on steps of Provincial Parliament Building at a rally in support of the preservation of Meares Island. Made a number of appearances on TV talk shows. Broadcast Christmas poem commissioned by CBC.

A Checklist

228 POETRY

Patmos and Other Poems, 1955, Routledge & Kegan Paul.

Third Day Lucky, 1958, Oxford University Press.

Two Ballads of the Muse, 1960, Rampant Lions Press, privately published*.

Begging the Dialect, 1960, Oxford University Press.

The Dark Window, 1962, Oxford University Press.

A Valedictory Poem, 1963, privately published*.

An Irish Gathering, 1964, Dolmen Press.

A Ballad of Billy Barker, 1965, Morriss Printing Co.*

Inscriptions, 1967, privately published.

Because Of This, 1968, Manchester Institute of Contemporary Arts*.

Selected Poems 1947-1967, 1968, McClelland and Stewart Limited.

The Hold of Our Hands, 1968, privately published*.

An Irish Album, 1969, Dolmen Press.

Georges Zuk: Selected Verse, 1969, Kayak.

Answers, 1969, Enitharmon Press.

The Hunting Dark, 1971, McClelland and Stewart Limited / André Deutsch.

Remembering Synge, 1971, Dolmen Press*.

A Different Mountain, 1971, Kayak.

A Private Speech, 1971, Sono Nis Press.

Three For Herself, 1972, Sceptre Press.

Musebook, 1972, Pharos Press.

A Christmas Poem, 1972, privately published*.

Country Songs, 1973, Sceptre Press*.

Timelight, 1974, McClelland and Stewart Limited / Heinemann Educational Books Ltd.

Fifty Syllables for a Fiftieth Birthday, 1975, privately published*.

Georges Zuk: The Underwear of the Unicorn, 1975, Oolichan Books.

Callsigns, 1976, Sono Nis Press.

Because of Love, 1977, McClelland and Stewart Limited.

Three Poems, 1977, Sceptre Press.

Landmarks, 1979, Sono Nis Press / Oolichan Books.

Collected Shorter Poems 1947-1977, 1981, Sono Nis Press.

Limits, 1981, Porcupine's Quill, Inc.

De Nihilo, 1982, Aloysius Press*.
Zuk, 1982, Porcupine's Quill, Inc.
Wordsong, 1983, Sono Nis Press.
Distances, 1985, Porcupine's Quill, Inc.
Collected Longer Poems, 1947-1977, 1985, Sono Nis Press.

VERSE TRANSLATIONS
Two Hundred Poems from the Greek Anthology, 1971,
    Washington University Press / McClelland and Stewart Limited
    / Methuen Publications.
George Faludy: Twelve Sonnets, 1983, Pharos Press.
George Faludy: Selected Poems 1933-1980, 1985, McClelland and
    Stewart Limited / University of Georgia Press.

DRAMA
The Paper Cage, 1983, Oolichan Books.

FICTION
The Man Who Sang in His Sleep, 1984, Porcupine's Quill, Inc.

BIOGRAPHY AND HISTORY
John Ruskin: The Final Years, 1955, Manchester University Press.
J.M. Synge and His World, 1971, Thames & Hudson.
They Call It The Cariboo, 1980, Sono Nis Press.

CRITICISM
The Poetic Pattern, 1956, Routledge & Kegan Paul.
Cavalier Poets, 1960, Longmans.
Teach Yourself Poetry, 1963, English University Press.
The Practice of Poetry, 1971, Heinemann Educational Books Ltd.
The Writings of J.M. Synge, 1971, Thames & Hudson.
J.M. Synge, 1972, Bucknell University Press.
The Poet's Calling, 1975, Heinemann Educational Books Ltd.
Poetic Truth, 1978, Heinemann Educational Books Ltd.

OCCULT
Spellcraft, 1978, McClelland and Stewart Limited.
Talismanic Magic, 1985, Samuel Weiser.

ART
Painters Talking, 1957, privately published*.
*Paintings, Graphics & Sculptures from the Collection of Robin
    and Sylvia Skelton*, 1971, privately published*.

The Limners, 1972, 1975, 1978, Pharos Press*.
Explorations Within a Landscape: New Porcelain by Robin Hopper, 1978, privately published*.
Herbert Siebner: A Monograph, 1979, Sono Nis Press.

House of Dreams, 1983, Porcupine's Quill, Inc.

EDITIONS

J.M. Synge: Translations, 1961, Dolmen Press.
J.M. Synge: Four Plays and The Aran Islands, 1962, Oxford University Press.
J.M. Synge: Collected Poems, 1962, Oxford University Press.
Edward Thomas: Selected Poems, 1962, Hutchinson & Co. (Publishers) Ltd.
Selected Poems of Byron, 1965, Heinemann Educational Books Ltd.
David Gascoyne: Collected Poems, 1965, Oxford University Press.
J.M. Synge: Riders To The Sea, 1969, Dolmen Press.
David Gascoyne: Collected Verse Translations (with Alan Clodd), 1970, Oxford University Press.
Synge / Petrarch, 1971, Dolmen Press.
The Collected Plays of Jack B. Yeats, 1971, Secker & Warburg.
Ezra Pound: From Syria, the Worksheets, Proofs and Text, 1981, Copper Canyon Press.

ANTHOLOGIES

Leeds University Poetry 1949, 1950, Lotus Press.
Six Irish Poets, 1962, Oxford University Press.
Poetry of the Thirties, 1964, Penguin Books Limited.
Five Poets of the Pacific Northwest, 1964, Washington University Press.
Viewpoint, 1962, Hutchinson & Co. (Publishers) Ltd.
Poetry of the Forties, 1968, Penguin Books Limited.
Introductions From an Island, 1969, University of Victoria*.
The Cavalier Poets, 1970, Faber.
Introductions From an Island, 1971, University of Victoria*.
Introductions From an Island, 1973, University of Victoria*.
Introductions From an Island, 1974, University of Victoria*.
Introductions From an Island, 1977, University of Victoria*.
Six Poets of British Columbia, 1980, Sono Nis Press.

SYMPOSIA

The World of W.B. Yeats (with Ann Saddlemyer), 1965, Dolmen Press / Washington University Press / Oxford University Press / The Adelphi Bookshop.

Irish Renaissance (with David Clark) 1965, Dolmen Press.
Herbert Read: A Memorial Symposium, 1970, Methuen
  Publications.

231

*pamphlets, chapbooks and broadsides

The Sixty Contributors

FLEUR ADCOCK is the author of many volumes of poetry, and of verse translations from the medieval Latin. Her *Selected Poems* appeared in 1983, and in the same year she edited the *Oxford Book of Contemporary New Zealand Poetry*. Born in New Zealand, she has lived in England for a number of years.

MARGARET ATWOOD's many books of poetry and fiction have brought her all the most important literary awards in Canada. Her most recent novel, *The Handmaid's Tale*, was published in 1985. She is an ex-chairperson of the Writers' Union of Canada.

JOHN BARTON's most recent book of poetry is *Hidden Structure* (1984). He studied in Skelton's poetry workshops at the University of Victoria.

EUGENE BENSON teaches at the University of Guelph and has published many works of fiction, drama, and literary criticism. He is also a librettist and for a number of years has been an organizer of the Guelph Spring Festival. He is an ex-chairman of the Writers' Union of Canada.

MARILYN BOWERING divides her time between writing poetry and fiction, and teaching at the University of Victoria where she was once Robin Skelton's student. Her most recent book is a volume of new and selected poetry, *The Sunday Before Winter*.

ROBERT BRINGHURST's *The Beauty of the Weapons: Selected Poems 1972-1982* appeared in 1982. Bringhurst is a typographer and book designer as well as a poet and translator. Winner of this year's CBC Poetry Competition he lives on Bowen Island in British Columbia.

PAMELA BARLOW BROOKS is a painter and calligrapher living in Victoria. Her animated movie, *Calligraphy*, has been shown in many parts of the USA and Canada, and has just been released in video.

VIRGIL BURNETT is a printmaker and book illustrator as well as a writer of fiction and a professor of Fine Arts at the University of Waterloo.

JUNE CALLWOOD is the author of many books of history and social criticism, and her articles on the status of women today have appeared in many newspapers and magazines. Her impressive *A Portrait of Canada* was published in 1981. She is an ex-chairperson of the Writers' Union of Canada.

TONY CONNOR's *New and Selected Poems* appeared from the

University of Georgia Press in 1982. He is a professor at Wesleyan University, though born in Salford, England, where he first met Skelton and joined him and Michael Seward Snow in founding first 'The Peterloo Group' of poets and painters, and later The

Manchester Institute of Contemporary Arts.

GEORGE CUOMO's most recent novel, *Family Honor,* was published in 1983. After teaching at the University of Victoria and then in California, he moved to New England where he is a professor at the University of Massachusetts.

A.M. CURRIE, OBE, is Secretary (Registrar) of the University of Edinburgh, Scotland.

MICHAEL ELCOCK is the Executive Director of Tourism Victoria, and has organized many arts festivals. His photographs have been widely published. He lives in Sooke, BC.

CHAD EVANS is a sixth-generation British Columbian, now living in Australia. He has written many articles on environmental issues for government and other publications. *Frontier Theatre,* his history of nineteenth-century theatrical entertainment in the Canadian far west and Alaska, appeared in 1983.

GEORGE FALUDY is generally recognized as Hungary's greatest poet. His *Selected Poems* 1933-1980, which Skelton edited and translated, appeared in 1985. He is a Canadian citizen and lives in Toronto.

GREG GATENBY directs the reading programme at Harbourfront, Toronto, and has been responsible for many international poetry festivals featuring writers from all over the world.

MAURICE GOOD is an actor / director who has appeared in many roles from Beckett to Shakespeare in most of the major theatres in Canada and Britain. His one-man shows, *John Synge Comes Next* and *The Ham in Sam,* have toured both Canada and Europe. *Every Inch a Lear,* his rehearsal journal of Ustinov's *Lear* at Stratford, Ontario, was published in 1983.

COLIN GRAHAM is Director Emeritus of the Art Gallery of Greater Victoria, which he developed from a small place with few facilities into a gallery of national importance. His monograph on Philip McCracken was published in 1980, and he has had many one-man exhibitions of his paintings.

RALPH GUSTAFSON's anthologies were the first to put modern Canadian poetry on the world map. His work has received many honours, and he is currently putting together a Collected Poems which will consolidate the work of fifty years. His most recent poetry collection is a volume of selected poems, *At the Ocean's Verge* (1984).

SAM HAMILL, together with Tree Swenson, founded and runs the Copper Canyon Press in Port Townsend, Washington. A poet as well as a printer and typographer, he has published many books.

LALA HEINE-KOEHN is a painter and poet. Her most recent collection of poems is *Forest Full of Rain*. She studied in Skelton's poetry workshops at the University of Victoria.

GEORGE HITCHCOCK is the founder-editor of the magazine *Kayak*. Well known as both poet and playwright, he is also an actor and director. He lives in Santa Cruz, California. His most recent publication is *October at the Lighthouse: Collected Stories* (1985).

GEOFFREY HOLLOWAY has published several collections of his poetry, the most recent being *The Crones of Aphrodite*. He lives and works in England's Lake District.

GEORGE JOHNSTON is celebrated internationally as a scholar and translator of Icelandic and Faroese poetry, as well as an award-winning poet. He recently retired from his professorship at Carleton University.

DIANE KEATING's most recent collection of poetry is *The Optic Heart* (1984) in which text is accompanied by drawings by the Montreal artist, Ingrid Style. She lives in Toronto.

LUELLA KERR has published several books of poetry and is also a painter. She lives in Victoria.

THOMAS KINSELLA has gained international renown not only as a poet but also as the translator of much Gaelic literature, including *the Táin*. He divides his time between the USA and Ireland, where he manages the Pepper Canister Press. He is a professor at Temple University.

G.R. WILSON KNIGHT died in Exeter, England on 20 March, 1985 at the age of 87. A fine actor, he played classic roles in both Canada and England, but his reputation rests chiefly upon such seminal works of Shakespearean criticism as *The Wheel of Fire* and *Shakespearean Production*. He taught at the University of Leeds, where Skelton was a student.

CHARLES LILLARD is a poet, critic, editor, bibliographer and an authority on British Columbia history. He has edited many historical journals and other works. His most recent book is *Seven Shillings a Year: A History of Vancouver Island*. He divides his time between writing and teaching at the University of Victoria.

KEITH MAILLARD's sequence of novels, *Two Strand River, Alex Driving South, The Knife in My Hands,* and *Cutting Through* was issued as a series in 1984 by General Publishing. Maillard is a musician as well as a novelist and teaches at the University of British Columbia.

LIAM MILLER's Dolmen Press has produced many of Ireland's finest books. He is also an authority on fine printing and has written many articles on the subject. Miller is an ex-president of the Irish Publishers' Association.

JOHN MONTAGUE is internationally known as one of Ireland's leading poets. His *Selected Poems* of 1982 was published simultaneously in Canada, Ireland, England and the USA. He teaches at the University of Cork but frequently visits both Canada and the USA.

CARL MORRIS's long career as a painter in the Pacific Northwest has been celebrated by the University of Oregon, which designed a special atrium to house a permanent collection of his work, and by Reed College, which has created its own special collection. He provided the sumi ink illustrations for Skelton's anthology, *Five Poets of the Pacific Northwest.*

HILDA MORRIS's sculptures are to be found in major buildings and public spaces in many parts of the USA. Some of her most recent pieces are *Winter Column,* in the Portland Art Museum, *Mountain Piece,* in the University of Rochester Memorial Gallery of the Rochester Museum, and *Wind Gate,* on permanent display with a number of her other works at Reed College.

SUSAN MUSGRAVE has published a novel, two books for children, and a number of broadsides and chapbooks as well as twelve volumes of poetry, the most recent being *Cocktails at the Mausoleum.* She lives on Vancouver Island where she is currently completing a second novel.

NORMAN NICHOLSON holds the Queen's Medal for Poetry, in addition to a number of other important awards. As well as poetry, he has published verse dramas, criticism, autobiography and topographical studies. His latest book, *Selected Poems 1940-1982,* was published by Faber.

ROBERT O'DRISCOLL is an editor and scholar of Irish literature. His monumental compilation, *The Celtic Consciousness,* was named Outstanding Academic Book of the Year in 1982, in the USA. He is Director of Celtic Studies at the University of Toronto, where he has organized many international conferences on Irish Studies.

MYFANWY PAVELIC's drawings, collages and paintings are to be found in many public galleries, including the National Gallery of Canada and England's National Portrait Gallery. Her most recent exhibition, *Relationships,* was presented at the North Park Gallery in Victoria, on the outskirts of which she lives. She is an RCA and has the Order of Canada.

KATHLEEN RAINE is not only renowned as one of England's senior poets, but also has an international reputation as a Blake and W.B. Yeats scholar. She is the founder and editor of the international magazine of the arts and the imagination, *Temenos*.

MARION RIPPON's four Crime Club novels are *The Hand of Solange, Behold the Druid Weeps, The Ninth Tentacle* and *Lucien's Tombs*. She is also the author of *Ahmi*, a novel set in the Canadian north. She lives in Victoria, BC.

PETER ROBINSON is a poet who has published his work in periodicals throughout Canada and the UK. He is a regular columnist for *Poetry Canada Review*, and he has recently completed his second detective novel for Penguin. He lives in Toronto.

LEON ROOKE's fiction has been published widely in both Canada and the USA. His most recent book is *A Bolt of White Cloth* (1984). He lives in Victoria, BC and spends some time teaching at the University of Victoria.

JOE ROSENBLATT's most recent volume of poems was the selection, *Poetry Hotel*, published in 1985 along with his first volume of memoirs, *Escape from the Glue Factory*. He has taught at a number of Canadian universities, and is a recipient of the Governor General's Award.

HERBERT SIEBNER's paintings, drawings, engravings and sculptures are as well known in Berlin and London as in Victoria, where he now lives. This year, a forty-year retrospective of his work is being mounted in Berlin. He is a member of the Royal Canadian Academy.

SYLVIA SKELTON is a calligrapher, and current chairman of the Fairbank Society of Calligraphers in Victoria BC. As Robin Skelton's wife, critic, tax-consultant and chief booster, she has both encouraged and enabled him to produce his long list of published books.

MICHAEL SEWARD SNOW founded 'The Peterloo Group' in Manchester with Tony Connor and Robin Skelton. A painter and sculptor, he has recently given up his teaching position at the Exeter School of Art in order to devote all his time to creative activity.

WILLIAM DAVID THOMAS has been a cattle rancher, merchant seaman, rose grower, university teacher and journalist. He is a Robert Graves scholar and has edited some of his work, as well as writing about him. An expert cook, he lives in Victoria, where he has recently completed a book on French cuisine.

FLORENCE VALE is an artist and the author of two collections of drawings and humorous verse, *Selected Drawings and Verse*

(1979) and *The Amorous Unicorn* (1984). A retrospective exhibition of her artwork toured Ontario's major galleries in 1980. She is a devout fan of the infamous French servant of Eros, Georges Zuk.

W.D. VALGARDSON is the Chairman of the Creative Writing Department at the University of Victoria. He has published three collections of short stories, a novel, *Gentle Sinners,* which won the 1981 Books in Canada first novel award, and a collection of poems.

SEÁN VIRGO is the author of two collections of short fiction and many volumes of poetry. He has received a number of awards for his short stories both in Canada and in England. A former student of Robin Skelton's, he is currently Writer-in-Residence at St. Jerome's College, University of Waterloo, where he is completing his first novel.

SUSAN WALKER is the publisher of *Quill & Quire,* of which she was the editor for many years. She is also the editor of the quarterly, *Canadian Art.* She lives in Toronto.

ANN WALSH is the author of *My Time, Your Time.* She lives in Williams Lake, BC where she is completing a second work of fiction.

DAVID WATMOUGH's fiction sequence reached its sixth volume in 1984 with the publication of *Fury.* He has performed his monodramas before many audiences across Canada, and was the founding president of the British Columbia Writers' Federation.

JOHN WEBB was teaching in the English Department of David Thompson University Centre in Nelson, BC at the time of its closure in 1984. He now lives, writes and teaches in Toronto. His poems have appeared in *Queen's Quarterly* and in the *Antigonish Review.*

MONCRIEFF WILLIAMSON recently retired as Curator of the Confederation Centre Art Gallery and Museum in Charlottetown, PEI. He is the author of *Robert Harris: Portraits,* a biography of the artist, and several thrillers, including *Through Canadian Eyes* (1976).

MARCIA MCNEILL WILLIS is a Canadian photographer living in Los Angeles. Her portraits of Robin Skelton have appeared in several of his books.

BRIAN WILSON is a trade union activist who lives and works in Toronto. He has long been a student of the Celtic consciousness, both in Canada and in Ireland itself.

CHRISTOPHER WISEMAN is a poet, critic and editor. His book on the work of Edwin Muir, *Beyond the Labyrinth* appeared in 1978.

He is currently consolidating his many books of poetry into a volume of collected poems. He teaches at the University of Calgary.

GEORGE WOODCOCK, Canada's senior man of letters, has published so many books of poetry, biography, travel, literary and social criticism that even he must have lost count. He was the founding editor of *Canadian Literature*. He has declined most awards, but accepted the Governor General's Award and the Molson Prize. His works have been translated into many languages.

LUDWIG ZELLER, poet and collagist, was born in Chile but now resides in Toronto, as a Canadian citizen. He has published many collections of poetry, and books and portfolios of his collages, which have received international awards.